SONOMA COUNTY

ITS BOUNTY II

Laguna

Recipes from
Sonoma County's Finest Chefs

ISBN: 9658701-1-1

Published by Ellen D. Moorehead
Petaluma CA 94952

CREDITS

Ellen D. Moorehead, Editor/Coordinator

Orienne Bennett, Recipe Formatting

Don Bennett, Copywriting and Editing; Book Consultant

E. Ross Parkerson, Sketches

Norman Gaddini, Scratch Board Art

Hal Moorehead, Expediting and Accounting

Scott Hess, Photography

Front Cover Credits: Scott Hess, photography; setting courtesy of Armida Winery; Sonoma County food products, Fiesta Market. Back Cover Credits: Scott Hess, photography; Sonoma County scenes.

WIMMER
COOKBOOKS

ConsolidatedGraphics

1-800-548-2537

TABLE OF CONTENTS

Articles about "Sonoma County – Its Bounty II" co-sponsors are located throughout the book. Without these essential Sonoma County restaurants, wineries and food producers, this cookbook would not have been possible.

ABOUT OUR ARTISTS

E. ROSS PARKERSON

The pen and ink sketches of Sonoma County buildings featured in this book are the work of artist E. Ross Parkerson. A career city planner, Parkerson became well known for his sketches of Petaluma's historical structures, many of which have been featured in annual calendars. He is a former member of the Petaluma City Council and a long-time advocate of preservation of historical structures. He and his wife Margaret now live in Corvallis, Oregon.

NORMAN GADDINI

The unique scratchboard artwork presented in this book is the work of Sonoma County artist Norman Gaddini. Accomplished in a number of artwork disciplines, Gaddini has been most highly acclaimed for his work in the scratchboard medium for the past 32 years. A native of Healdsburg and a long-time resident of Sebastopol, Gaddini has won numerous awards for his creations. Both he and his work can be seen at his gallery in Occidental.

Donkeys on Jovine Road
(Norman's Home)

ACKNOWLEDGMENTS

When a book such as this reaches completion, the Editor recalls its inception and the people who made it possible. This includes the Co-Sponsors and recipe contributors.

The owners and board of Directors of Clover-Stornetta Farms have been supportive of the project. I thank them and Dan Benedetti, President, who has worked with us whenever we needed his help and guidance.

Clover not only has special products, they have special people working for them. Betty Visser, Martha Kuhn, and Renée Norris are among those who contributed to this effort.

Thank you Orienne Bennett, Don Bennett, E. Ross Parkerson, Hal Moorehead, and Norman Gaddini for working to make the cookbook a reality. Norman, a multi-talented artist and a special person, was introduced to us by another special friend, Ann Maurice. One of Ann's contributions was to be Clo's assistant in creating SMOOTHIES.

Appreciation goes to Joe DeVito, Council For Community Television, Bob Clark, Clark Video Productions, for their promotion of Sonoma County...Its Bounty I and II.

Last, but not least, I am grateful for the help of Vincent McAllister, Alison Moorehead, and Barbara Meconitas.

We are happy to present this new book to you for enjoyment with family and friends.

Ellen D. Moorehead

Editor, Publisher

Norman Gaddini's "Experience the Bounty" is published with permission of and thanks to the Sonoma County Harvest Fair Board of Directors. "Experience the Bounty" was their 1999 Harvest Fair Poster. (see page 10)

CLOVER'S NORTH COAST
EXCELLENCE PROGRAM

A decade ago Clover-Stornetta decided to differentiate their product from the commodity called milk. With a strong emphasis on quality, Clover-Stornetta introduced the North Coast Excellence program in 1995, with full third party certification in 1999. Through the NCE program Clover has succeeded in answering questions of concern as they pertain to social responsibility and environmental and economic viability. As a result of their efforts, Clover has been quoted as having "quite possibly the cleanest milk in the United States."

The North Coast Excellence Program has four aspects. The first is quality. Clover maintains the highest standards based on Somatic Cell Count, Standard Plate Count, Lab Pasteurized Count, and On-Farm Temperature Watch. The second deals with the use of rBST. Clover cows are not treated with the growth hormone rBST. All of our ranchers sign an affidavit stating that they do not treat their cows with this growth hormone. The third aspect of the NCE program is ranch appearance. The clean appearance of Clover's ranches reflects the superior milk products being produced within. Clover's ranchers maintain 90% ranch scores, and continually upgrade their dairies. The fourth aspect of the NCE program is Clover's ongoing commitment to foster sustainable agriculture. Within that context Clover was the first processor to have all of their dairy partners complete detailed farm plans. The assertions Clover make regarding the NCE program are audited annually by a certified public accounting firm.

Clover Stornetta has a commitment to provide the highest quality dairy products to their consumers, to insure the welfare of their herds, and to promote progressive sustainable agriculture practices. As a result, Clover Stornetta and their dairy farmers were the first dairy operation in the U.S. to be awarded the Free Farmed label from the American Humane Association. As of March, 2003, Clover is the only California dairy with this certification, which means that Clover cows are free from unnecessary fear and distress, and are ensured conditions and care that limit stress. Clover cows are also free from unnecessary pain, injury and disease, free from hunger and thirst, assured ample shelter, and free to enjoy their lives by sharing company with their own kind.

ORGANICS

Most of Clover's organic milk comes from St. Anthony's Farm, located 10 miles west of Petaluma. St. Anthony's Farm is a residential drug and alcohol recovery program with a working organic dairy. As a Franciscan operation, it recognizes the inherent dignity of each person and fosters relationships based on respect.

This philosophy naturally translates into respect for the earth. St. Anthony's Farm cows get a diet of 100% organically grown feed which is produced using only organically approved fertilizers and pest control. These cows are not treated with antibiotics or the bovine growth hormone rBST.

St. Anthony's milking herd is approximately 230 cows, which is smaller than the average California herd size, with ample pasture. Clover also receives organic milk from four dairy families in Humboldt and Del Norte Counties.

Clover is committed to family farming, sustainable agriculture, and providing the highest quality milk products by creating the best possible environment for their herds. All of this combines to make Clover Stornetta Milk the "Milk of Human Kindness." Whether you enjoy Clover's line of conventional or organic dairy products, you can enjoy them in good conscience and good health.

The partners of Clover Stornetta Farms include Gene Benedetti, Gary Imm, John Markusen, Dan Benedetti, Herm Benedetti, Mike Keefer and Kevin Imm. They salute you, the consumer, for your support. "Tip Clo through your two lips!"

From Left Upper Row: Gary Imm, Lynn Imm, Kevin Imm, John Markusen, Mike Keefer, Anne Benedetti, Dan Benedetti, Herm Benedetti, Paul Ross
From Left Lower Row: Pat Markusen, Evelyn Benedetti, Diane Keefer, Gene Benedetti, Marilyn Benedetti, Lois Ross
(Mary Imm not pictured)

FOREWORD

In recent years, Sonoma County has become a national leader in the development of agricultural practices that take special care to preserve our land for future generations, take extra care in overseeing the health of farm animals, protect watersheds, and many other practices designed to deliver our agricultural resources to future generations substantially unaltered. This practice is called sustainability.

This dedication to maintaining the integrity of our land and its resources has drawn the attention of many others with a commitment to quality foodstuffs - chefs, restaurant owners, food processors, and farmers, among others. This single-minded dedication to quality has made Sonoma County a number one supplier of quality food items to the Bay Area restaurant industry, from fine lamb, chickens and turkeys to sought-after vegetables of many kinds.

The rewards of this commitment to the land come in the form of some of the finest produce, meats and dairy products available anywhere, and some of the world's best chefs dedicated to showcasing these products at their absolute finest.

Accordingly, Clover-Stornetta takes great pride in being a part of presenting this second volume of the best recipes from the best food producers and food preparers in Sonoma County. We have a tremendous "Bounty of Sonoma County" because our people truly care. May you enjoy the dishes presented in these pages.

Dante Benedetti, President
Clover-Stornetta Farms, Inc.

Experience the Bounty

THE BOUNTY OF SONOMA COUNTY

"I firmly believe, from what I have seen, that this is the chosen spot of all the earth as far as Nature is concerned." Luther Burbank, discussing Sonoma County.

Ask almost anyone who lives here, and they'll tell you Sonoma County is one of the world's finest places to live.

Sonoma County has beauty, variety, a temperate climate, some of the world's finest wines, a rich history, and agricultural abundance and diversity.

About beauty - Sonoma County has a magnificent Pacific coastline, priceless towering redwood groves, mountains, and emerald green hills in mid-winter.

About the climate - Sonoma County, because it seldom drops below freezing in the winter, boasts green hills in January, and summers cooled by the ocean fog. This distinctly Mediterranean climate contributes to the high quality of Sonoma County's ag products.

About diversity - the County's southern region boasts dairies, the western region produces some of America's most sought-after seafood, and much of the County features world-class vineyards. The Sebastopol area is home to the famed Gravenstein apple. Truck farms, small organic vegetable farms and greenhouses grow produce for the Bay Area's finest restaurants are everywhere, and finest-quality poultry and lamb are also found throughout Sonoma County. Small organic vegetable farms and greenhouses that now provide produce daily to the area's best restaurants. A range of microclimates enables Sonoma County to produce not just a wide variety of outstanding wine grapes, but also other sought-after agricultural products.

About fine wines - Sonoma County has major wine regions, which produce outstanding varietal wines, with more than a hundred wineries open to the public.

About history - England's Sir Francis Drake sailed the Sonoma Coast and the imperial expansions of both Russia and Spain met here in the early 1800's. The Sonoma Mission, the northernmost of the Spanish missions, was founded to counter Russia's settlement at Fort Ross. Subsequently, the Sonoma settlement was the site of the famed Bear Flag revolt, where American settlers declared their independence from Mexico and set in motion a chain of events that led to California's annexation by the United States.

Because of all of the above, Sonoma County is a popular destination for 7.1 million visitors a year. Foremost among them are moviemakers, who have been using the geographical and architectural backdrops and quaint settings for movies since days of the silents. Alfred Hitchcock chose Santa Rosa for Shadow of a Doubt because of its all-American qualities, and returned for The Birds. George Lucas chose Petaluma for American Graffiti (as did Francis Ford Coppola for Peggy Sue Got Married.) In recent years, movies shot here include Mumford, Lolita, Bandits, Cheaper by the Dozen, Animal, Inventing the Abbotts, and more. Directors shooting TV commercials have become a mainstay of the Sonoma County landscape.

Perhaps Sonoma County's greatest visitor attraction, however, is its food. Because so much high quality produce, poultry, seafood, and meat is grown here for the Bay Area's best restaurants, it was inevitable that the County would develop its own restaurants to rival the best the Bay Area had to offer. Throughout Sonoma County, from the cities to the smallest villages, excellent restaurant choices are available.

In this book, we have gone to these outstanding chefs and asked them to share their know-how in converting the "bounty of Sonoma County" into truly memorable feasts.

Miss Sonoma Cownty

My Forest

MENUS

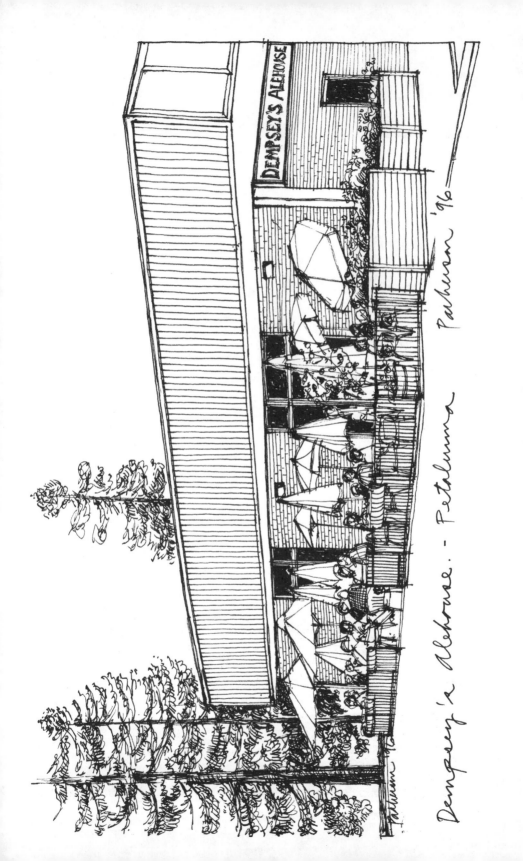

Dempsey's Alehouse. - Petaluma   Parkinson '96

CHEF BERNADETTE BURRELL, DEMPSEY'S RESTAURANT AND BREWERY

These dishes can be prepared as a complete multi-course dinner or individually for light summer eating.

Arugula Salad with Lemon Champagne
Vinaigrette and Goat Cheese

Mussels Española

Roasted Marinated Chicken
with Southern Corn Pudding

Dessert: My favorite sweet is a big bowl of
Clover Ice Cream with fresh berries on top

ARUGULA SALAD WITH LEMON CHAMPAGNE VINAIGRETTE

Arugula is a full flavored green. It has flavors of pepper and is a little spicy on the palate; it blends beautifully with the Lemon-Champagne Vinaigrette. Dempsey's has a farm located at Red Rooster Ranch. We grow lots of arugula, and other greens for the restaurant.

½ cup champagne vinegar
1½ cups olive oil
Zest of ¼ lemon
¼ cup sliced garlic

¼ cup sliced shallots
6 tablespoons finely diced flat
  leaf parsley
Salt and pepper to taste

Place champagne vinegar in a bowl, slowly add olive oil. Add the rest of the ingredients and mix well. Season to taste. Store in airtight container in refrigerator. It keeps for 2 weeks.

For 2 cups of arugula, toss with ½ ounce of dressing, place on platter and garnish with your favorite local goat cheese.

2¼ cups vinaigrette

ROMESCO

This sauce can be used as a base for many different items. We use ours on sandwiches, to top fish or chicken, or to finish a sauce as used in the mussels. I like it smeared on flat bread as a tasty little treat.

3 dried chiles de arbol, seeded
  and stemmed
1 red bell pepper, roasted,
  peeled and chopped
½ cup roasted tomatoes
¼ cup olive oil

¼ cup toasted hazelnuts
¼ cup toasted almonds
¼ cup chopped parsley
½ cup toasted dried bread
1 ounce red wine vinegar

Soften chiles in warm water for ½ hour. While chiles are soaking, gather other ingredients. In the bowl of a food processor, place red peppers, roasted tomatoes and olive oil. Blend to a fine paste and remove from bowl. Add rest of ingredients to the bowl of the food processor and blend to an almost fine paste. Add ingredients together in a bowl and combine well.

MUSSELS ESPAÑOLA

8-10 mussels per person
2 tablespoons extra virgin
  olive oil
2 ounces white wine

2 tablespoons romesco sauce
3 tablespoons water
Lemon wedges and parsley for
  garnish

Wash mussels and scrub the outside of the shells. Most fishmongers will have washed and scrubbed their mussels, you can ask if they will need additional scrubbing. Place olive oil in saucepot, place your burner flame on medium, add white wine and reduce wine by ½. Add romesco sauce, mussels and water. Cover pot and gently cook until all mussels are open. Remove pot from heat and lift mussels to a serving tray. Taste sauce and adjust the salt and pepper. Garnish with lemon wedges and sprinkle with chopped parsley.

CORN PUDDING

This corn pudding is not going to win any dietary awards, but it sure is tasty. We make this pudding ahead and when it cools, cut it into squares and heat it when we have an order. It will keep up to a week in the refrigerator.

3 cups corn cut off the cob
  (you can substitute frozen,
  but must drain the liquid)
1½ cups diced yellow onions
½ cup diced red bell pepper
2 tablespoons chopped garlic
4 tablespoons olive oil
9 eggs
1½ cups milk

3 cups heavy cream
2 tablespoons Worcestershire
  sauce
1 tablespoon salt
½ tablespoon white pepper
¼ cup sugar
¾ cup Asiago cheese, grated
¾ cup cornmeal
2 teaspoons cayenne

Preheat oven to 350 degrees. In a sauté pan over low heat, gently sauté the corn, onions, peppers and garlic in olive oil. While that is sautéing place eggs, milk, cream in a large bowl. Whip together until well incorporated. Add Worcestershire sauce, salt, pepper and sugar. In a separate bowl mix Asiago and cornmeal with cayenne. Gently stir cornmeal mixture into cream mixture, blending well. Add all ingredients from sauté pan and stir. Place in 9½-inch baking pan. Bake at 350 degrees for 45 minutes until the mixture is set up and when you shake the pan the mixture is not loose.

ROASTED CHICKEN

This marinade takes a little bit of time because of the lemon juice.
You can make this up to a week in advance. It will make enough
marinade for 2 or 3 chickens. The more marinade you put on the
chicken, the more robust in flavor.

1 cup lemon juice	1 teaspoon cayenne
¼ cup garlic	¼ cup black pepper
2 teaspoons cumin	½ cup kosher salt
1 tablespoon cinnamon	¾ cup honey
2½ tablespoons paprika	1½ tablespoons dried oregano

Put all ingredients together in a large plastic container and mix
well. If you have a hand blender, blend thoroughly. Place cut up
chicken in marinade. It is best if it sits overnight.

Roast chicken at 350 degrees for 1 hour or until chicken ex-
trudes clear liquid when poked with a knife. Save pan drippings
for sauce.

SAUCE FOR CHICKEN

4 onions, julienne	3 pints chicken stock
2 tablespoons chopped garlic	5 pieces apricots (dried) cut
½ tablespoon good quality	into pieces
paprika	Pan drippings from roasted
	chicken

Gently sauté onions and garlic until translucent. Add rest of
ingredients, simmer until reduced by ½. Season to taste.

CHEF DAN DABBAS,
ESSA'S RESTAURANT

Oysters in Champagne Sauce

Sonoma Mixed Greens with Sonoma Jack Cheese

Chicken Provençale

Apple and Pear Bruschetta

OYSTERS IN CHAMPAGNE SAUCE

The champagne butter sauce is a perfect foil for the briny flavor of the oysters, and the sprinkling of salty prosciutto and crunchy pistachios adds textural contrasts to the silky oysters.

Rock salt for serving
20 oysters, shucked
¼ cup sliced prosciutto, cut
    into ⅙-inch julienne

¼ cup chopped pistachio nuts
4 chervil sprigs
Champagne Sauce
    (recipe follows)

CHAMPAGNE SAUCE

1 tablespoon minced shallot
½ cup dry champagne
2 tablespoons champagne
    vinegar
½ cup heavy cream

4 tablespoons unsalted butter,
    cut into small pieces
Salt and freshly ground white
    pepper to taste

Place the shallot, champagne and vinegar in a small sauce pan over medium heat. Bring to a boil and reduce by ⅓. Add the cream to the pan and reduce again by ⅓. Remove the pan from the heat but keep the burner on low. Whisk in the butter 1 piece at a time. Season with salt and pepper.

To serve: Place a bed of rock salt in each of 4 dishes and arrange 5 oysters on each plate. Sprinkle with proscuitto and pistachios. Garnish with chervil sprig. Serve with Champagne Sauce.

4 servings

SONOMA MIXED GREENS WITH SONOMA JACK CHEESE

2 tomatoes, chopped into
    small cubes
1 red onion, finely chopped
9 ounces Sonoma Jack cheese,
    cubed ½-inch

7 ounces mixed salad greens
1 teaspoon honey
1¼ cups extra virgin olive oil
Juice of 1 lemon
Salt and pepper

Mix tomato and onion together in a bowl with the cheese and add the salad greens. Prepare the dressing by mixing the honey, olive oil, lemon juice, salt and pepper. Pour the dressing over the salad, mix gently. Serve on chilled plates.

4 servings

CHICKEN PROVENÇALE

4 single chicken breasts 8-10
   ounces each
Salt and pepper
4 tablespoons olive oil
2 cups sliced mushrooms
2 tablespoons minced garlic
2 tablespoons minced shallots

1 cup chopped tomato, peeled
   and seeded
20 pitted kalamata olives
1 cup white wine
½ cup cold butter
4 tablespoons chopped herbs
   (parsley, chive and thyme)

Bone chicken breasts. Season with salt and pepper. Sauté chicken in olive oil 15 minutes until golden brown and completely cooked. Remove from pan and keep warm. Add mushrooms and cook for 5 minutes. Add garlic and shallot and cook for 1 minute. Add tomato and olives and cook for 1 minute. Add wine and reduce by ½. Adjust seasoning. Finish the sauce with butter and herbs. Pour sauce over chicken.

4 servings

APPLE AND PEARS BRUSCHETTA

4 vanilla beans, divided
1 Granny Smith apple,
   quartered and cored
1 pear, quartered and cored
1 cup sugar

1 cup Riesling wine
1 loaf sourdough bread
½ stick butter
Crème fraîche
Mint sprigs

Purée 1 vanilla bean and sugar in a food processor. Place apple and pear in a bowl. Sprinkle the sugar on top, pour in the wine and macerate for 20 minutes. Heat oven to 400 degrees. Butter 6 ovenproof bowls. Cut ½-inch thick slices from the bread and spread with butter. Place a piece of bread, butter side up in each bowl. Top with fruit mixture and bake 15 to 20 minutes. Warm crème fraîche and drizzle over each bowl. Garnish with mint and ½ vanilla bean.

4 servings

CHEF JEFFREY MADURA, JOHN ASH & COMPANY

Spring Menu From the Best of Sonoma County

Fresh Pea Soup with Tarragon and Fennel Oil

Asparagus Salad with Pickled Ginger Vinaigrette

Rosie's Organic Chicken Breast
Steamed in Cabbage with a Cider Cream Sauce

Roasted Pork Loin Salad
Stuffed with Caramelized Fennel, Red Onion and Watercress,
Served with Orange and Pink Peppercorn Vinaigrette

CK Leg of Lamb Stuffed
with Wild Mushrooms and Figs

Grandma's Blackberry Cobbler
with Clover-Stornetta Vanilla Ice Cream

FRESH PEA SOUP
WITH TARRAGON AND FENNEL OIL

*Recommended wine: The fresh licorice flavor from the tarragon is a
great link to the Ferrari-Carano Fumé Blanc.*

1 tablespoon unsalted butter
1 cup chopped onions
1 cup chopped leeks, both
    white and tender green
    parts
½ cup chopped celery
¼ cup chopped carrot
3½ cups rich vegetable or
    chicken stock
½ cup dry white wine

4 cups shelled fresh peas
1 cup loosely packed tarragon
    leaves
3 cups loosely packed and
    finely sliced romaine or
    other green lettuce
Kosher salt and freshly ground
    black pepper
Garnish: Fresh tarragon leaves
    and fennel oil

In a medium saucepan, melt the butter. Add the onions, leeks,
celery, and carrot. Sauté until soft but not browned. Add the
stock and wine. Bring to a boil. Reduce the heat and simmer for
10 minutes. Add the peas and tarragon. Simmer for 5 minutes
longer or until the peas are soft. Add the lettuce and simmer for
2 minutes or until the lettuce is just wilted and tender. Transfer
to a blender or food processor, in batches if necessary, and purée
the soup. Strain and return the soup to the saucepan. Bring back
to a simmer and season to taste with salt and pepper. Serve
garnished with fresh tarragon leaves and a drizzle of fennel oil.

6 servings

ROSIE'S ORGANIC CHICKEN BREASTS

Steamed in Cabbage with Cider Cream Sauce

Recommended wine: The slightly spicy and tart apple note of this superb chicken dish can be beautifully paired with Ferrari-Carano Chardonnay.

4-8 large leaves green cabbage
3 tablespoons unsalted butter
   or olive oil
2 cups peeled and sliced tart
   apples, cut approximately
   ¼-inch thick
2 tablespoons slivered shallots
1 teaspoon high-quality curry
   powder
Kosher salt

Freshly ground black pepper
4 6-ounce boneless, skinless
   Rosie's chicken breast
   halves
1 cup thinly sliced mushrooms
⅓ cup dry white wine
Garnish: Roasted baby carrots
   and onions, fresh thyme
   leaves

Make Cider Cream Sauce and set aside (recipe follows).

In lightly salted boiling water, briefly blanch the cabbage leaves, about 30 seconds. Remove and plunge immediately into ice water to stop the cooking, then drain and set aside. In a medium sauté pan, heat 2 tablespoons of the butter or oil and sauté the apples and shallots until tender. Add the curry powder and sauté until fragrant, approximately 1 to 2 minutes. Season with salt and pepper.

Divide the sautéed apples among the 4 cabbage leaves. Place a chicken breast on top of the apple mixture and fold over the cabbage leaves to completely enclose. If necessary, place a second cabbage leaf around the mixture. In a large sauté pan, heat the remaining tablespoon of butter or oil. Add the sliced mushrooms and sauté 1 minute. Place the cabbage packets on top of the mushrooms, add the wine, cover and steam over moderate heat for 7 to 10 minutes or until the breasts are just done but moist.

To serve, remove the cabbage packets and mushrooms with a slotted spoon and place on warm plates on a pool of Cider Cream Sauce. Garnish with the baby vegetables and a scattering of thyme leaves.

4 servings

CIDER CREAM SAUCE

5 tablespoons unsalted butter at room temperature
½ cup sliced mushrooms
1½ cups minced green onions, white part only
1 cup peeled, cored and roughly chopped tart apples

⅔ cup apple cider or ⅓ cup applejack brandy
2 cups rich chicken stock
1 tablespoon fresh lemon juice
¾ cup heavy cream
1 tablespoon drained green peppercorns

In a medium saucepan, heat 1 tablespoon of the butter and sauté the mushrooms, green onions and apples until lightly browned. Add the cider or brandy, stock and lemon juice and reduce by half. Add the cream and reduce to a light sauce consistency. Remove from the heat, whisk in the remaining 4 tablespoons of butter, and strain the sauce. Slightly crush the green peppercorns and add to the sauce, which can be kept warm in a thermos for up to 3 hours.

ASPARAGUS SALAD WITH PICKLED GINGER VINAIGRETTE

Recommended wine: Ferrari-Carano Fumé Blanc will contrast with the spicy rush of ginger in this dressing.

1 teaspoon chopped shallots
2 tablespoons chopped pickled ginger (available in Asian markets)
¼ teaspoon wasabi powder

2 teaspoons rice wine vinegar
4 tablespoons dark sesame oil
1½ pounds fresh asparagus
Kosher salt and freshly ground black pepper

Prepare a charcoal fire. In a small bowl, combine the shallots, pickled ginger, wasabi powder, rice wine vinegar and sesame oil. Whisk thoroughly to blend. Season to taste with salt and pepper. Brush the asparagus with some of the vinaigrette. Grill the asparagus over hot coals until bright green and tender. Serve the asparagus drizzled with the remaining vinaigrette.

2 to 3 servings

LEG OF LAMB STUFFED
WITH WILD MUSHROOMS AND FIGS

Recommended wine: This is a rich, full-flavored dish that goes well with the Ferrari-Carano Tresor.

Olive oil
½ cup finely chopped shallots
   or green onions, both white
   and pale green parts
½ cup finely chopped carrots
¼ cup finely chopped celery
2 tablespoons finely chopped
   garlic
1 cup coarsely chopped shiitake
   or cremini mushrooms
½ cup lightly toasted pine nuts
⅓ cup chopped dried figs or
   pitted prunes

⅓ cup bulgur wheat
¼ cup loosely packed fresh
   mint, chopped
1 teaspoon each chopped fresh
   thyme and rosemary
2 teaspoons grated lemon zest
1¼ pounds ground lamb
1 egg, lightly beaten
Salt and freshly ground black
   pepper
1 8 to 9 pound leg of lamb,
   boned

RED WINE DEGLAZING SAUCE

⅔ cup diced onion
⅔ cup diced carrots
⅔ cup diced celery
3 garlic cloves, diced
1 cup hearty red wine

2½ cups rich chicken or
   mushroom stock
2 tablespoons finely chopped
   fresh parsley

Preheat oven to 500 degrees. In a medium sauté pan, heat 3 tablespoons olive oil. Add shallots, carrots, celery, garlic and mushrooms until lightly colored. Remove from heat and transfer to a bowl. Stir in pine nuts, figs, bulgur, mint, thyme, rosemary and lemon zest. Allow the mixture to cool completely, then mix in the ground lamb and egg. Season with salt and pepper. It's a good idea to sauté a tablespoonful to taste for seasoning since this filling can't be tasted raw. Season the cavity of the leg of lamb with freshly ground pepper. Sew the small end of the leg with a trussing needle and twine or a skewer to close. Spoon the stuffing into the cavity and sew or skewer the opening to enclose the stuffing completely. With kitchen twine, tie the leg securely at 2-inch intervals. Rub the lamb generously with olive oil and season well with salt and pepper.

Place the lamb on a rack in a roasting pan in the middle of the oven and roast for 10 minutes. Reduce the heat to 375 degrees and roast for another 30 minutes. At this time, scatter the diced onions, carrots, celery and garlic cloves for the red wine deglazing sauce in the bottom of the pan. The lamb should continue to cook for about another 45 minutes until medium rare or until an instant-read thermometer registers 125 degrees in the thickest part of the leg. When the meat is done, transfer the lamb to a serving platter and cover very loosely with foil to keep warm.

DEGLAZING SAUCE
Place the roasting pan over high heat and add the wine and stock. Boil for 6 to 8 minutes to reduce, scraping up any browned bits from the bottom of the pan. Carefully strain and degrease the sauce and season with salt and pepper. Stir in the chopped parsley. Serve the lamb cut into ¼-inch slices with sauce spooned around the lamb.

8 to 10 servings

Tomales

ROASTED PORK LOIN SALAD

Stuffed with Caramelized Fennel, Red Onion and Watercress
Served with an Orange and Pink Peppercorn Vinaigrette

6 6-ounce pork tenderloins
3 tablespoons clarified butter
   or olive oil
1 medium fennel bulb, cored
   and cut into ¼-inch dice
1 medium red onion, cut into
   ¼-inch dice

2 bunches watercress leaves,
   washed and picked and cut
   in julienne strips
Ground black pepper to taste
Kosher salt to taste
¼ cup olive oil

After cleaning and trimming pork tenderloin, place sharpening steel into center of tenderloin and create a pocket for stuffing. In a large sauté pan, heat clarified butter until hot. Add diced fennel and red onion and coat well with butter. Caramelize the onion mixture at high flame for 8 to 12 minutes. Once caramelized, cool mixture down. Once cooled, add watercress and season with salt and pepper, mix well. Then take mixture and stuff ¼ cup of each mixture into each pork tenderloin cavity. Once all are stuffed, marinate in olive oil and salt and pepper until ready to cook. Heat sauté pan with olive oil or heat grill and cook pork tenderloins until medium, about 8 to 10 minutes. Once cooked, let stand to retain juices and heat. While tenderloin sits, make salad and dressing.

SALAD AND DRESSING

2 medium fennel bulbs, thinly
   sliced vertically in ¹⁄₁₆-inch
   slices
2 medium red onions, thinly
   sliced in rings and shocked
   in water for 10 minutes

2 bunches watercress,
   stemmed and cleaned
2 blood or navel oranges,
   peeled and sliced into thin
   rounds ¼-inch thick
Kosher salt and ground black
   pepper

Arrange salad by mixing shaved fennel, red onion and watercress in stainless steel bowl. Add salt and pepper to taste and arrange attractively on 6 large platters. Then add orange rounds to each bunch to give height.

Cut tenderloin into 6 pieces and arrange next to salad mixture. Drizzle with Orange and Pink Peppercorn Vinaigrette (recipe to follow) and garnish with fennel frond.

6 servings

ORANGE AND PINK PEPPERCORN VINAIGRETTE

6 ounces unsweetened frozen
orange juice concentrate
⅓ cup low sodium soy sauce
¼ cup rice wine vinegar
1 tablespoon peeled and
minced fresh ginger
1½ teaspoons dark sesame oil

½ cup chopped green onions,
white and pale green parts
¼ cup chopped fresh Italian
flat leaf parsley
1 cup olive or peanut oil
¼ cup dry toasted pink
peppercorns

In a food processor or blender, combine all ingredients except the oil and pink peppercorns. Process until smooth. Transfer to a bowl. Stir in the oil and peppercorns, being careful not to emulsify; otherwise the dressing will be too thick. Store any unused dressing, covered and refrigerated, for up to 2 weeks.

GRANDMA'S BLACKBERRY COBBLER

4 pounds fresh blackberries
1 cup sugar
1¼ cups flour, or combination
of rolled oats and flour
1 cup pecans or walnuts

⅓ cup dark brown sugar
1 teaspoon ground ginger
1 teaspoon ground cinnamon
½ cup very cold unsalted
butter, cut in cubes

Toss blackberries with 1 cup sugar and ¼ cup of the flour. Pour into an ovenproof dish and smooth the surface. In food processor, pulse pecans, remaining cup of flour, brown sugar, spices and butter. Sprinkle mixture over fruit in pan. Bake in preheated 350 degree oven for 45 minutes. Serve warm or at room temperature with a dollop of vanilla ice cream.

6 to 8 servings

ZiN
RESTAURANT. & WINE BAR

Parkeren '02

Zin Restaurant

CHEF JEFF MALL, ZIN RESTAURANT

Zinful Dinner for 6

Roasted Pear Salad
with Prosciutto, Blue Cheese and Toasted Walnuts
in Honey Lemon Vinaigrette

❖⟶◉⟵❖

Coq au "Zin" Served Over
Celery Root Mashed Potatoes

❖⟶◉⟵❖

Applejack Apple Pie with
Vanilla Ice Cream

CELERY ROOT MASHED POTATOES

1 celery root (about
   1¼ pounds), peeled and
   cut into ½-inch cubes
1 cup heavy cream
4 tablespoons unsalted butter

2 pounds Idaho potatoes,
   peeled and cut into quarters
1 tablespoon kosher salt
Fresh ground black pepper

Place celery root, cream and butter together in sauce pot with lid. Bring to a boil then simmer over low heat. Cook for 30 minutes or until celery root is soft. Place potatoes in pot and cover with cold water. Add salt and bring to a boil. Simmer for 20 minutes until cooked. Drain potatoes in a colander and combine with celery root and cream in a mixer. Mash together until combined. Season to taste with salt and pepper.

6 servings

ROASTED PEAR SALAD

with Prosciutto, Blue Cheese and Toasted Walnuts in Honey Lemon Vinaigrette

3 Bosc pears, peeled, cut in half and cored
1 tablespoon sugar
2 ounces prosciutto ham, sliced thin and cut into small pieces

¾ cup walnut pieces, toasted lightly
6 ounces blue cheese crumbled
1 head frisée or curly endive, rinsed and cut
Salt and fresh ground pepper to taste

HONEY LEMON VINAIGRETTE

2 lemons, zested and juiced
1 tablespoon champagne vinegar
1 tablespoon honey
1 teaspoon Dijon mustard

½ teaspoon salt
¼ teaspoon fresh ground black pepper
2 drops Tabasco sauce
¾ cup virgin olive oil

Preheat oven to 450 degrees. Toss the pear halves in sugar and place on baking sheet. Bake 25 minutes, or until pears are golden brown. Set aside until ready to make salad.

Make vinaigrette: Place lemon zest and juice, vinegar, honey, mustard, salt, pepper and Tabasco sauce in blender. With motor running, slowly add oil in a steady stream until emulsified.

Assemble salad: Cut pears into slices and place in mixing bowl with prosciutto, walnuts, blue cheese and frisée. Toss lightly and add dressing as needed. Season to taste with salt and pepper.

6 appetizer servings

COQ AU "ZIN"

6 slices "Applewood Smoked" bacon
¼ cup pure olive oil
12 chicken thighs (leave skin on but remove any excess fat)
Kosher salt
Fresh ground black pepper
1 cup flour
2 tablespoons minced fresh shallots
1 teaspoon minced fresh garlic
1 teaspoon minced fresh marjoram
2 cups broiler onions
2 cups cremini mushrooms, cleaned, stemmed and quartered
1 750 ml bottle Zinfandel (preferably Sonoma County)
2 cups chicken stock
1 bunch thinly sliced chives

Preheat oven to 350 degrees. Dice bacon into ½-inch pieces and render in heavy bottom sauté pan until crisp. Drain bacon fat from the pan and add olive oil. Return to medium heat. Season chicken with salt and pepper and dredge in flour. Sear chicken in the olive oil until well browned on both sides. Cook the chicken in small batches. Remove seared chicken to a 9 x 13-inch ovenproof casserole dish. Drain all but 2 tablespoons of fat from the pan. Add shallots, garlic and marjoram and sauté for 1 minute. Add onions and mushrooms to pan. Deglaze pan with the wine. Scrape bottom of pan to release the browned bits. Add chicken stock and bacon. Bring to a boil. Pour red wine mixture over chicken and cover tightly with foil or lid. Place in oven for 45 minutes.

Remove chicken from casserole, strain mushrooms, onion and bacon from sauce and reserve. Return sauce to stove top in a small sauce pan, bring to boil, reduce to simmer and cook until sauce is reduced by ⅓. Place chicken on platter, spoon mushroom, bacon and onion mixture over top, and ladle sauce around. Sprinkle with fresh minced chives.

6 servings

APPLEJACK APPLE PIE

5 Gravenstein or Granny
   Smith apples
1 teaspoon ground cinnamon
2 teaspoons fresh lime juice

1½ ounces applejack apple
   brandy
⅔ cup granulated sugar
2 ounces butter

PIE CRUST

3 cups all purpose flour
1½ teaspoons salt
1 cup vegetable shortening

½-¾ cup ice water
1 tablespoon sugar

To prepare crust: Combine the flour, salt and shortening in a mixing bowl and cut with two knives until the mixture is crumbly. Add the water slowly until the mixture begins to come together. Do not overwork the dough. Gather it into a ball and sprinkle with a few more drops of water if needed. Divide ball in half. Flatten each piece into a disk, wrap in plastic and chill for 30 minutes before rolling out.

To prepare filling: Peel, core and slice the apples thin. Toss in a bowl with the cinnamon, lime juice, applejack and sugar. Roll out both crusts. Lay bottom crust in 9-inch round Pyrex pie plate. Place ½ of the apple mixture in the pie pan. Dot the apples with ½ of the butter. Add the remaining apples and juice. Dot the apples with the remaining butter. Cover apple mixture with the top crust. Crimp the edges together and poke several steam holes in the top. Sprinkle top crust with water and 1 tablespoon sugar. Place the pie in a preheated 400 degree oven until the pie starts to bubble. Lower the temperature to 350 degrees and bake for 1 hour, or until the crust is brown and the apples are tender. Let cool before cutting.

Serve with vanilla ice cream and/or warm caramel sauce.

6 servings

CHEF BARBARA HOM,
JELLYFISH RESTAURANT,
SHERATON PETALUMA HOTEL

*Ravioli of Shiitake Mushrooms, Duck Confit
and Goat Cheese with Primavera Sauce*

*Salmon Corn Cakes on Bed of Frisée
with Lemon Grass Aïoli*

*Star Anise Petaluma Liberty Duck Breast
with Cherry Berry Sauce*

*Caramelized Pear with
Lemon Mascarpone and Gingersnaps*

RAVIOLI OF SHIITAKE MUSHROOMS, DUCK CONFIT AND GOAT CHEESE WITH PRIMAVERA SAUCE

FILLING

¾ cup sautéed shiitake
   mushrooms
¾ cup shredded duck confit
1 cup goat cheese

1 egg
1 teaspoon nutmeg
Salt and pepper to taste

Mix above ingredients.

RAVIOLI

1 egg
1 teaspoon water

1 package wonton skins

Scramble egg and water in a bowl to use as glue. Paint 1 won ton skin with egg mix. Drop a spoonful of goat cheese mix in center of won ton skin. Cover with another skin. Pinch to close. Place on floured parchment while you complete the rest. Drop in boiling water for 4 minutes. Drain and serve with Primavera Sauce.

PRIMAVERA SAUCE

10 Roma tomatoes
2 tablespoons olive oil
1 tablespoon chopped garlic

1 tablespoon chopped basil
Salt and pepper to taste

Blanch, peel, de-seed and roughly dice tomatoes. Heat oil in sauté pan. Add garlic and sauté for 2 minutes. Add tomatoes and sauté for 3 minutes. Add basil and sauté for 1 minute. Pour sauce over cooked raviolis.

4 servings

SALMON CORN CAKES ON BED OF FRISÉE WITH LEMON GRASS AÏOLI

LEMON GRASS AÏOLI
4 stalks lemon grass
1 cup light corn oil
2 egg yolks

Juice of 1 lemon
 (about 1 tablespoon)

Roughly chop the tender part of lemon grass stalks. Put in blender with oil and purée. Heat mixture until very hot but not smoking and remove from heat. Let sit for a day or two and then strain. Put 2 egg yolks in blender along with lemon juice. Slowly add lemon grass infused oil until emulsified.

SALMON CORN CAKES
2 cups roughly puréed salmon
    scraps
½ cup corn kernels
¼ cup finely diced red peppers
1 egg
¼ cup finely chopped onion

2 tablespoons chopped cilantro
1 teaspoon salt
¼ teaspoon white pepper
½ cup panko (Japanese
    breadcrumbs)
1 tablespoon olive oil

Mix all ingredients except olive oil and form into 3-inch round cakes about 1-inch thick. Sauté cakes in olive oil for 2 to 3 minutes on each side. Drain.

TO SERVE
Toss frisée (or other hearty salad greens) with salt and a little extra virgin olive oil. Place frisée on individual plates and place salmon cakes on bed of greens. Drizzle with lemon grass aïoli.

4 servings

STAR ANISE PETALUMA LIBERTY DUCK BREAST WITH CHERRY BERRY SAUCE

MARINADE

½ cup soy sauce
1 tablespoon ginger
1 tablespoon cilantro
1 tablespoon chopped green
  onions
1 tablespoon honey

3 whole star anise
1 tablespoon minced orange
  peel
1 tablespoon minced garlic
1 cup cherry cider reduced to
  ½ cup

Place above ingredients in blender and blend.

GRILLED DUCK BREASTS

4 Liberty duck breasts
  (Trim off skin about
  ¼ around the breast and
  marinate overnight.)
¼ cup shallots

½ cup red wine (preferably the
  wine that will be served
  with dinner)
Strained marinade from above
¼ cup soft butter

Place duck breast, skin side down in sauté pan over very low heat. Pour grease off as fat starts to melt. Continue for 15 minutes. (Duck should not be actually cooking.) In the meantime, strain the marinade. Sauté the chopped shallot. Deglaze with red wine. Add the strained marinade. Heat for 2 minutes and then whip in the soft butter. When ready to serve, turn flame to medium high and flip breasts over. Cook for 3 minutes until duck is medium rare. Slice at an angle and ladle Cherry Berry Sauce over.

CHERRY BERRY SAUCE

⅓ cup cherries
⅓ cup raspberries
⅓ cup blackberries
4 tablespoons chopped shallots

½ cup Pinot Noir
1 cup duck stock
½ cup butter, divided

Place berries in blender and purée. Strain seeds out and set mixture aside. Sauté shallots in 2 tablespoons of the butter until golden. Deglaze with Pinot until reduced by ½. Add duck stock and reduce by ½ again. Add the berry purée. Whip in remainder of the butter and serve.

4 servings

CARAMELIZED PEAR WITH LEMON MASCARPONE AND GINGERSNAPS

CARAMELIZED PEAR

2 ripe pears ¼ cup butter
¼ cup sugar

Peel, cut in half and core the pears. Toss with the sugar. Heat butter in nonstick sauté pan. Add pear and slowly sauté until nice and caramelized on both sides (about 10 minutes). Cut and fan pears and place on a serving plate.

LEMON CURD

Zest of 2 lemons Pinch of salt
¾ cup lemon juice 10 egg yolks
1 cup sugar 4 ounces butter

Combine all ingredients except butter. Cook slowly in non-aluminum pan (cook like crème anglaise) stirring constantly. When it starts to thicken, whisk in butter. Chill.

LEMON MASCARPONE

⅓ cup mascarpone 4 sprigs mint
⅓ cup lemon curd 4 gingersnaps
4 strawberries

Whip mascarpone until stiff. Fold in lemon curd. Dollop or pipe on top of the caramelized pears. Garnish with strawberry, mint and gingersnaps.

4 servings

CHEF SCOTT SNYDER, SASSAFRAS

A Winter Menu at Sassafras

Spicy Crab Cakes with Louisiana Tartar Sauce

Braised Leg of Muscovy Duck
with Figs, Olives and Pinot Noir

Green Salad, Shaker-Style

Meyer Lemon Cheesecake
with Cranberry Compote

CRAB CAKES WITH
LOUISIANA TARTAR SAUCE

¼ cup unsalted butter
¼ cup flour
1 cup milk
½ teaspoon cayenne
1 teaspoon salt
1 pound Dungeness crabmeat,
  drained and picked over to
  remove bits of shell

¼ cup chopped flat-leaf parsley
¼ cup chopped green onion
1 cup flour
Tabasco sauce and lemon juice
  to taste, if desired
3 eggs
3 cups breadcrumbs
4 tablespoons vegetable oil

Combine butter and flour in a saucepan and cook briefly,
stirring with a whisk. Pour in milk, whisking. Add the cayenne
and salt. Simmer until thickened and smooth, whisking frequently.
Pour into a large mixing bowl and cool to room temperature.
Mix in crabmeat, green onions and combine thoroughly. Add
Tabasco and lemon juice if desired. Divide mixture into 12
portions. Form these into fat discs. Bread by rolling first in flour,
then beaten egg, then breadcrumbs. Chill for at least 2 hours.
Fry the cakes on both sides in the oil in a heavy skillet, abut
5 minutes. Serve with the tartar sauce, lemon wedges and a
lightly dressed cabbage and watercress salad.

6 servings

LOUISIANA TARTAR SAUCE

2 cups mayonnaise, preferably
  homemade
1 tablespoon Creole mustard
¼ teaspoon cayenne
1½ teaspoons salt

½ cup finely chopped scallions
½ cup finely chopped flat-leaf
  parsley
½ cup finely chopped
  cornichons

Combine all ingredients. Adjust to taste with lemon juice and
Tabasco.

BRAISED LEG OF MUSCOVY DUCK WITH FIGS AND OLIVES

¾ cup dried Black Mission
   figs, halved
2 cups Pinot Noir
1½ cups pitted black olives,
   kalamata or oil-cured, soaked
   briefly, rinsed and dried
6 Muscovy duck legs, about
   12 ounces each

Salt and pepper to taste
¼ cup olive oil
½ cup sliced shallots
2 cups duck, chicken or veal
   stock
2 tablespoons butter
½ cup minced parsley

Soak figs in wine several hours. Preheat oven to 350 degrees.
Trim excess fat from duck legs, season with salt and pepper.
Brown legs in oil on both sides and place in an ovenproof
casserole with a tight-fitting lid. Combine wine, figs and shallots
in the pan the duck was browned in, bring to a boil and pour
over the duck. Cover the casserole and place in preheated oven.
Braise the duck for 1½ to 2 hours until tender. Check by pierc-
ing a leg with a small sharp knife. Drain the liquid in the
casserole into a saucepan. Remove as much fat from the surface
as possible with a spoon or small ladle. Add the stock to the
liquid and boil until reduced to sauce-like consistency. Swirl in
the butter, add the parsley and pour over the duck, figs, olives
and shallots. Serve immediately.

Good with spoonbread flavored with pumpkin purée.

6 servings

GREEN SALAD, SHAKER-STYLE

3 tablespoons tarragon vinegar
1 tablespoon minced onion
1½ teaspoons chopped fresh
  thyme
1½ teaspoons chopped fresh
  savory
1½ teaspoons chopped fresh
  tarragon
½ teaspoon dry mustard
1 teaspoon salt
Freshly ground black pepper
½ cup olive oil

½ pound Blue Lake beans or
  haricots verts, trimmed,
  washed, blanched until
  crisp-tender and chilled
3 heads Bibb or Boston
  lettuce, trimmed, washed,
  dried and torn into large
  pieces
2 tablespoons green onion,
  sliced
1 small red onion, thinly sliced
¼ pound mushrooms,
  extremely fresh, rinsed,
  wiped dry and thinly sliced

Combine vinegar, onion, herbs, mustard, salt and pepper in a
serving bowl. Slowly whisk in olive oil to emulsify. Add all other
ingredients and toss gently but thoroughly. Serve immediately.

6 servings

Sebastopol Siesta

MEYER LEMON CHEESECAKE WITH CRANBERRY COMPOTE

CRUST

2 cups gingersnap crumbs,
  preferably homemade

3 tablespoons melted butter
2 tablespoons soft butter

Combine the crumbs and melted butter. With the softened butter, grease a 9-inch springform cake pan. Press an even layer of the crumb mixture onto the bottom of the pan. Refrigerate.

FILLING

1½ pounds cream cheese,
  softened
1¼ cups sugar
6 egg yolks
1 pint sour cream

6 tablespoons flour
2 teaspoons vanilla extract
⅓ cup Meyer lemon juice
Grated rind of 2 Meyer lemons
6 egg whites

Preheat oven to 350 degrees. Cream the cheese in a large mixing bowl. Beat in the sugar. Beat in the yolks one at a time. Stir in sour cream, flour, vanilla, lemon juice and rind. Beat the egg whites in a separate bowl with a whisk or electric beater until stiff but not dry. With a rubber spatula, fold the whites gently into the cream cheese mixture.

Pour the filling into the cake pan, smoothing the top with a rubber spatula. Wrap the bottom and sides with plastic wrap, then aluminum foil. Lower the wrapped pan into a shallow baking pan and fill the baking pan with hot water until it is halfway up the side of the cake pan. Bake for approximately 1 hour until the center is just set, yet still somewhat soft. Cool or chill to serve.

COMPOTE

6 ounces fresh cranberries
½ cup sugar

Zest of 1 orange
Juice of 1 orange

Combine all ingredients and bring to a simmer. Cook until reduced to sauce consistency, about 15 minutes. Cool to room temperature.

Serve the cheesecake with the compote and garnish with whipped cream and/or candied lemon peel.

CHEF JOSH SILVERS, SYRAH

*Crab and Avocado Salad
with Chilled Tomato Soup*

Pan Roasted Sonoma Duck Breast
with Mascarpone Polenta and Blackberry Gastrique

Mascarpone Cheesecake

CRAB AND AVOCADO SALAD

2 avocados, diced
8 ounces crabmeat
1 teaspoon minced shallot
1 teaspoon chopped tarragon

1 ounce rice wine vinegar
2 ounces olive oil
Salt and pepper to taste

Add all and mix. Place Chilled Tomato Soup in a bowl, garnish with about an ounce of salad and serve.

12 servings

CHILLED TOMATO SOUP

1 yellow onion
2 stalks celery, sliced
6 cloves garlic
Olive oil
½ gallon chopped fresh tomatoes

½ gallon chicken stock
1 cup white wine
Salt and pepper
Sugar if needed

Sauté onion, celery and garlic in olive oil for about 10 minutes.
Add tomatoes and cook 5 to 10 minutes. Add stock. Simmer for
20 minutes. Blend with salt and pepper. Add sugar to taste. Chill.

1 gallon of soup

PAN ROASTED SONOMA DUCK BREAST

with Mascarpone Polenta and Blackberry Gastrique

1 duck breast
1 teaspoon peanut oil
½ cup chicken stock
½ cup cream
½ cup polenta
1 tablespoon mascarpone

1 tablespoon Parmigiano-
  Reggiano
3 tablespoons butter, divided
Salt and pepper to taste
1 tablespoon sugar
¼ cup blackberry vinegar
Blackberries for garnish

Method for Duck: Trim excess fat and score skin in diamond
pattern. Do not cut the meat. Sear breast in peanut oil, fat side
down. When brown, turn over and cook 30 seconds, turn over
again and place in hot oven (450 degrees) for 4 to 6 minutes.
Remove and let rest.

Method for Polenta: Bring stock and cream to a boil, add
polenta, stir until done. Add mascarpone, Parmigiano-Reggiano
and 1 tablespoon of butter. Salt and pepper to taste.

Method for Gastrique: Heat sauté pan until hot, add sugar and
caramelize. Add blackberry vinegar and reduce until a syrup-like
consistency. Mount with 2 tablespoons of butter and add
blackberries. Salt and pepper to taste.

To Serve: Slice duck breast thinly against the grain. Place the
polenta in the middle of a plate and cover with thin slices of
duck, pour gastrique over the duck and serve.

1 serving

MASCARPONE CHEESECAKE

CRUST
1 box vanilla wafers   6 ounces unsalted butter

Preheat oven to 350 degrees. Put wafers in food processor and grind until fine. Remove and place in a small bowl. Add butter and mix. Remove and set aside ¾ cup of mixture and place the remaining mixture in a 9-inch springform pan and press mixture to form crust approximately ⅛-inch thick. Place pan on cookie sheet and bake for 10 minutes. Let cool for 15 minutes.

FILLING
20 ounces natural cream   3 large eggs
   cheese   1 teaspoon vanilla extract
8 ounces mascarpone cheese   1 teaspoon fresh lemon juice
1 cup sugar   Pinch of salt

Mix cheeses and sugar in mixer for 2 minutes. Add eggs (one at a time), vanilla, lemon juice and salt. Stop occasionally to scrape the sides of the bowl. Put mixture in crust, place in the center of the oven and bake for 25 to 35 minutes at 350 degrees. (Mixture should look solid and slightly jiggle.) Remove from oven and cool for 20 minutes.

TOPPING
1 cup sour cream   1 teaspoon fresh lemon juice
¼ cup sugar   Pinch of salt
1 teaspoon vanilla

Mix all ingredients in a bowl and pour over cheesecake. Bake cheesecake for 10 more minutes. Remove from the oven and sprinkle with reserved cookie mixture. Chill for at least 6 hours before serving.

Note: For best results when cutting cheesecake, use a long thin knife and run under hot water, cleaning blade after each cut.

                                                    8 servings

CHEF MICHAEL QUIGLEY, CAFÉ LOLO

Dungeness Crab Tostadas
with Avocado Relish and Salsa

Coriander-Cured Lamb
with Dried Cherry-Zinfandel Sauce
and Basil Mashed Potatoes

Chocolate Kiss

DUNGENESS CRAB TOSTADAS

with Avocado Relish and Salsa

8 white corn tortillas, 3-inches in diameter   ¼ cup oil

CRABMEAT

8 ounces fresh lump crabmeat
2 tablespoons heavy cream

1 scant tablespoon fresh mayonnaise

CABBAGE SALAD

¼ head white cabbage
¼ cup sour cream
1 tablespoon lime juice

2 small serrano chiles, seeded and finely chopped
Salt and pepper

AVOCADO RELISH

2 ripe avocados (8 ounces each - California)
½ cup finely chopped red bell pepper
1 tablespoon minced serrano chile (may substitute jalapeño)

1 bunch cilantro
2 tablespoons lime juice
2 tablespoons hazelnut oil
1 teaspoon salt
Pepper to taste

TOMATO SALSA

2 cups chopped ripe plum
   tomatoes
½ cup minced red onion
1 bunch cilantro, chopped
   (¾ cup), reserve some
   leaves for garnish

2 teaspoons minced serrano
   chile (may substitute
   jalapeño)
2 tablespoons lime juice
1 teaspoon salt
Pepper to taste

Crabmeat: Pick through crabmeat to be sure it is free of any pieces of shells. In a mixing bowl, combine the crabmeat, cream and mayonnaise. Gently blend but do not overwork the mixture. The crabmeat should not become too finely shredded and pasty.

Cabbage salad: Very finely slice the cabbage. Blend the sour cream, lime juice and chiles in a bowl until smooth. Add the cabbage and mix until the cabbage is coated with sour cream. Salt and pepper to taste.

Avocado relish: Split and seed the avocados. Remove the skin. Cut the avocados into very small cubes. In a mixing bowl, combine the chopped avocado and red bell pepper, red onion, chile, cilantro, hazelnut oil and lime juice. Thoroughly mix the ingredients to form a coarse relish. Salt and pepper to taste.

Tomato salsa: Finely chop the tomatoes. Combine with onion, cilantro and chile. Add the lime juice and mix thoroughly. Salt and pepper to taste.

Tortillas: Cut 3-inch tortilla rounds from commercially available white corn tortillas. In a small skillet, heat ¼ cup of oil until very hot. Fry the tortillas until golden brown and crisp. Do not overcrowd the pan when frying the tortillas.

Assembly: Spread some of the cabbage mixture on the crisp tortilla. Layer some of the avocado relish over the cabbage. Place some crabmeat on the avocado relish and top the crabmeat with tomato salsa. Garnish the tostadas with cilantro leaves.

4 appetizer servings

Café Lolo

Parhram '94

CORIANDER-CURED LAMB

with Dried Cherry-Zinfandel Sauce and Basil Mashed Potatoes

6 tablespoons coriander seeds
6 tablespoons black
  peppercorns
6 shallots, minced
6 garlic cloves, minced
½ cup kosher salt
9 tablespoons dark brown sugar

½ cup olive oil
6 pounds lamb top sirloin
3 tablespoons vegetable oil
Dried Cherry-Zinfandel Sauce
  (recipe follows)
Basil Mashed Potatoes
  (recipe follows)

Place the coriander and peppercorns in the bowl of a food
processor and process for about 1 minute until coarsely ground.
Add the shallots, garlic, salt and sugar. With the machine
running, drizzle in the olive oil to make a thick paste. Transfer
to a large glass bowl and add the lamb to cure for at least 3 hours,
turning occasionally.

Preheat the oven to 400 degrees. Heat the vegetable oil in a
skillet over medium heat until lightly smoking. Remove the
lamb from the cure and scrape clean. Season with salt and sear
on all sides in the skillet. Transfer to an ovenproof baking dish
and cook for about 15 to 18 minutes for medium rare. When the
lamb is done, remove from the oven and let rest for 3 to 5 minutes.

Slice the lamb and serve with the Dried Cherry-Zinfandel
Sauce. Arrange the lamb slices on top of the sauce and serve
with the Basil Mashed Potatoes.

DRIED CHERRY-ZINFANDEL SAUCE

2 cups Zinfandel
¼ cup sugar
3 tablespoons red wine vinegar
1 quart veal stock

1 cup dried cherries
Salt and pepper to taste
1 cup sautéed wild mushrooms

Combine Zinfandel, sugar and vinegar in a saucepan over
medium heat and let reduce until syrupy. Add the veal stock
and simmer until reduced by ⅓. Add the cherries and simmer
another 10 minutes. Season with salt and pepper. Add mushrooms and simmer 2 more minutes.

BASIL MASHED POTATOES

1 bunch basil
½ cup olive oil

9 cups mashed potatoes (fully prepared with milk and butter)
Salt and pepper to taste

Blanch basil in boiling water for 5 seconds and drop immediately into ice water. Squeeze basil completely dry in a towel. Chop basil and place into a blender. Turn on blender and slowly add olive oil until gone. Mix basil purée into mashed potatoes until incorporated. Add salt and pepper as needed.

CHOCOLATE KISS

6 ounces semisweet chocolate
1 cup butter
3 eggs
3 egg yolks

⅓ cup sugar
5 ounces flour
¼ cup powdered sugar
¾ cup fresh raspberries

Melt chocolate in butter over a double boiler. Meanwhile whisk eggs, yolks and sugar in a mixer on medium speed for 10 minutes. Add melted chocolate to mixture and slowly add flour and whisk for 5 additional minutes. Prepare 6 ramekins or large ovenproof soup cups by coating with thin layer of butter and flour. Divide chocolate mixture equally into dishes and bake in 350 degree oven. After 6 minutes in oven, turn the baking sheet around and bake an additional 6 minutes. Kisses should be slightly runny in appearance. Turn onto serving plate, garnish with powdered sugar and fresh raspberries.

6 servings

CHEF COREY BASSO, LE BISTRO

Roma Tomato and Goat Cheese Salad

Parmesan Crusted Prawns
with Green Olive Pesto

Banana Fritters with
Easy Caramel Sauce and Vanilla Ice Cream

ROMA TOMATO
AND GOAT CHEESE SALAD

Roma tomatoes, 2 per person
Goat cheese, one ½-inch round
Salt and cracked black pepper
Extra virgin olive oil
10 year old balsamic vinegar or older
Sweet basil, cut in chiffonade

Slice tomatoes crosswise and fan in circle on plate. Place a goat cheese slice in the middle of circle. Season with salt and pepper. Drizzle with olive oil and balsamic vinegar. Place basil chiffonade on tomatoes and cheese.

PARMESAN CRUSTED PRAWNS WITH GREEN OLIVE PESTO

PESTO

2 garlic cloves
½ cup sweet basil
¼ cup pine nuts
¼ cup grated Parmesan cheese

6-8 green olives
Olive oil
Salt and pepper to taste

Blend garlic cloves, basil, pine nuts, Parmesan cheese and green olives in blender. Slowly add olive oil until smooth. (It is best to leave pesto loose to drizzle around prawns). Add salt and pepper.

PRAWNS

4-5 tiger prawns per person
   (I use U-15 size, under
   15 per pound)
Olive oil

Dijon mustard
Grated Parmesan cheese
Flour

Preheat oven to 400 degrees. Coat bottom of nonstick sauté pan with olive oil and heat until hot. Brush prawns with Dijon mustard, coat with cheese and then dust with flour. Add prawns to oil and sear until golden brown and crispy. Turn prawns and place pan in oven until prawns are cooked through, about 3 to 4 minutes.

Present prawns on rice, mashed potatoes, sautéed spinach, etc. Drizzle pesto around prawns and a little on top.

BANANA FRITTERS
WITH EASY CARAMEL SAUCE AND
VANILLA ICE CREAM

Bananas (just ripe is best) ½ per person, cut in half and then cut
  in half lengthwise

BATTER
½ cup flour   1 pinch cinnamon
½ cup powdered sugar   Half-and-half

Combine flour, powdered sugar and cinnamon in a bowl. Add
half-and-half until batter is creamy.

CARAMEL SAUCE
1 cup brown sugar   ¼ cup cream
2 tablespoons butter   2 tablespoons water

Bring all ingredients to a boil in a saucepan. Whisk while
boiling, about 2 to 3 minutes. Cool slightly.

TO COOK BANANAS
Place bananas in batter. Fry in nonstick sauté pan with clarified
butter or margarine. Cook until crispy and golden brown on
each side.

PRESENTATION
Place 2 pieces of bananas in bowl with scoop of vanilla ice
cream. Drizzle with caramel sauce.

CHEFS DAN AND KATHLEEN BERMAN, MIXX RESTAURANT

Basil Fettuccine
with Smoked Chicken, Niçoise Olives,
Poached Garlic & Sun-Dried Tomatoes

❖≈⊃€≈❖

Wilted Spinach Salad with Aged Wine Vinaigrette

❖≈⊃€≈❖

North Coast King Salmon Filet
with Lemon-Chanterelle Mushroom Sauce

❖≈⊃€≈❖

Middleton Farm Peach and Blackberry Crisp

BASIL FETTUCCINE

with Smoked Chicken, Niçoise Olives, Poached Garlic & Sun-Dried Tomatoes

This dish has been served at Mixx since the day we opened. It is the only item that has been on every menu for 13 years. I can often tell how many of our local regular customers are dining by how many Basil Fettuccine's I cook. We could never take this dish off the menu.

1 ounce unsalted butter
4-5 cloves garlic
6-8 pitted niçoise olives
5 sun-dried tomato halves
2 ounces white wine
2 ounces chicken stock

3 ounces cream
2 ounces smoked chicken,
  diced large
3 ounces basil-garlic fettuccine
2-3 leaves fresh basil, julienne

Heat butter in skillet. Add garlic, olives and tomatoes. Stir about 2 minutes. Do not brown. Add wine. Scrape pan and reduce by half. Add chicken stock. Bring to a boil and reduce by half. Add cream. Bring to a boil, reduce by half or until sauce coats the back of a spoon. Add chicken and toss together. Season to taste with salt and pepper. Meanwhile, cook pasta in boiling water 2 to 3 minutes, or until done. Drain and add to skillet. Toss to coat. Serve on a warm plate and garnish.

1 serving

WILTED SPINACH SALAD

4 ounces bacon, sliced thin
  and rendered
2 cups picked spinach leaves,
  stemmed
¼-½ cup red onion, sliced thin

2 ounces Aged Red Wine
  Vinaigrette (recipe follows)
Salt and pepper
2 ounces chèvre

Render fat from bacon. Put spinach and red onion in a large mixing bowl. Put bacon in sauté pan. Warm lightly. Add vinaigrette, heat quickly and adjust for seasoning. Add to spinach and toss lightly. Add cheese. Toss lightly and divide evenly on 2 plates. Serve at room temperature.

2 servings

AGED RED WINE VINAIGRETTE

2 cups aged red wine vinegar
2 tablespoons whole grain
   mustard
1 teaspoon ground pepper

2 teaspoons kosher salt
1 teaspoon sugar
8 cups pomace olive oil

Whisk all ingredients, except pomace, in mixer. Slowly add oil. Check seasoning.

NORTH COAST KING SALMON FILET

with Lemon-Chanterelle Mushroom Sauce

1 tablespoon peanut oil
   (or other hot burning oil)
2 6-ounce king salmon filets
Salt and pepper
Flour to lightly coat fish
1 tablespoon unsalted butter
4 ounces chanterelle or wild
   mushrooms, sliced
½ teaspoon garlic, diced
½ teaspoon shallots, diced

2 ounces Chardonnay
2 ounces fish stock (may
   substitute light chicken
   stock)
4 ounces heavy cream
Zest and juice from 1 lemon
   (Meyer lemon would be
   best)
1 teaspoon chopped parsley

Heat oil in skillet until almost smoking. Lightly dust fish in flour after seasoning with salt and pepper. Gently shake off excess flour. Place fish in skillet and sauté until golden, about 2 minutes. Turn fish over and do the same on the other side. Remove from pan, place on plate, cover and keep in a warm place. Pour excess oil out of skillet. Add butter and allow to bubble. Add mushrooms and sauté over medium heat until mushrooms render juices. Add garlic and shallots and sauté until soft, 1 to 2 minutes. Add Chardonnay, bring to boil and reduce by half, about 2 minutes. Add fish stock, boil and reduce by half, about 2 minutes. Add cream, boil and reduce until sauce lightly coats back of spoon. Add 1 tablespoon lemon juice, parsley and season with salt and pepper.

Presentation: Place king salmon filet on 2 warm plates. Divide sauce evenly in a diagonal fashion over fish. Garnish.

2 servings

FARM PEACH AND BLACKBERRY CRISP

Pastry Chef, Kathleen Berman

6-8 large peaches	1 tablespoon cornstarch
1¼ cups sugar	2 baskets blackberries

Peel and slice peaches into large pieces. Place in a large saucepan. Mix sugar and cornstarch with a whisk in a bowl. Sift mixture through strainer into the saucepan with peaches. Heat peaches, stirring with a rubber spatula only until sugar dissolves. Spoon into individual ramekins, leaving room for about 8 blackberries. Disperse blackberries by hand among the peaches. Place ramekins on sheet pan.

TOPPING

6 ounces dark brown sugar	½ ounce cinnamon
6 ounces granulated sugar	1 teaspoon salt
1¼ pounds unsalted butter	1 pound all purpose flour
1½ teaspoons vanilla	

Cream first 4 ingredients with a paddle in a kitchen-aide mixer. Sift next 3 ingredients and add to mixture. Mix until combined. Do not over-mix or topping will clump together.

Sprinkle topping over filled ramekins. Bake at 350 degrees, until topping is light brown and filling is bubbling.

6 to 8 large servings

CHEF BRIAN GERRITSEN,
APPLEWOOD INN AND RESTAURANT

Grilled Eggplant Soup with Parmesan Cheese

Simple Sliced Tomatoes
with Red Pepper Fondue and Local Olive Oil

*Whole Roasted Pork Loin Cured in our
Own Pressed Apple Cider*

Orchard Peach Ice Cream

GRILLED EGGPLANT SOUP WITH PARMESAN CHEESE

4 large globe eggplants (about 1 pound each)

½ medium white onion, small dice

3 cloves garlic, minced

2 sprigs marjoram

1 bay leaf

2 tablespoons extra virgin olive oil

⅔ cup white wine

6 cups cold water

Salt to taste

Juice of 1 lemon

¼ pound wedge Parmesan Reggiano

Prepare a hot coal fire over a grill and place the whole eggplant directly on the grill. Continue to cook the eggplant, turning occasionally, until the skins are charred and the flesh is tender. Cool slightly, then peel eggplant. Sauté onions and garlic with marjoram and bay leaves very slowly in olive oil over medium low heat until very tender. Add the white wine and reduce to a glaze. Add the eggplant, water and a generous amount of salt to taste. Bring to a simmer and cook about 15 minutes. Add the lemon juice and purée in a blender until smooth. Adjust the seasoning and serve in warm bowls with Parmesan shavings cut with a vegetable peeler.

6 servings

SIMPLE SLICED TOMATOES

with Red Pepper Fondue and Local Olive Oil

FOR THE RED PEPPER FONDUE

6 red bell peppers, washed   Salt
1 tablespoon extra virgin olive
    oil

Prepare a hot coal fire under a grill. Rub the peppers with olive oil and a generous sprinkling of salt. Grill the peppers about 5 minutes on each side, charring the skins slightly, but not burning them. Transfer to a bowl and cover with plastic film. Allow the peppers to steam for 10 minutes, then while still warm, peel and seed the peppers thoroughly. Cut the roasted peppers into small dice, then with a very sharp knife, continue to chop until the pepper is almost a purée. Transfer to a small strainer and allow the purée to drain any excess liquid. The purée should be quite thick. Reserve.

FOR THE DISH

6 large vine ripened heirloom
    tomatoes
Coarse sea salt and freshly
    cracked black pepper

The leaves from several
    springs of lemon thyme
3 tablespoons finest Sonoma
    County extra virgin olive
    oil (DaVero or McEvoy)

Bring a pot of water to a boil. Have on hand a bowl full of ice cold water. Submerge the tomatoes in the boiling water for 10 seconds exactly, then transfer to the cold water. Peel the tomatoes and slice each horizontally into 3 thick slices. Season all the tomatoes with sea salt, black pepper and a few lemon thyme leaves.

On each of 6 plates, stack 3 slices of tomatoes. Place a spoonful of red pepper fondue on each plate. Drizzle olive oil over the plates and garnish with remaining lemon thyme leaves.

6 servings

WHOLE ROASTED PORK LOIN

Cured in our Own Pressed Apple cider

For maximum flavor, allow the pork to cure in the brine for a full 48 hours.

FOR THE PORK

1 4-5 pound pork loin, boned and trimmed of any excess fat

Salt and freshly ground black pepper
2 tablespoons olive oil

FOR THE BRINE MIXTURE

2 quarts fresh pressed apple cider
4 quarts water
½ cup sugar
¼ cup kosher salt

1 tablespoon each toasted coriander and fennel seeds
1 teaspoon chili flakes
1 tablespoon black peppercorns
3 large sprigs fresh thyme

Combine all ingredients for the brine in a large non-reactive pot. Bring to a simmer and remove from heat. Allow to steep for 30 minutes, then cool in an ice bath. Place the pork loin in a container large enough to submerge it and pour the cooled brine over the pork. Make sure the entire loin is submerged, use a heavy plate if necessary. Cover the container and place in the refrigerator at least 24 hours and up to 48 hours to cure.

Remove the pork from the brine and discard liquid. Dry the pork loin with a clean cloth and season generously with salt and freshly ground black pepper. Allow the pork to come to room temperature, about 30 minutes.

Heat the oven to 375 degrees. Drizzle olive oil over the loin, place in a roasting pan and roast in the oven about 45 minutes for medium (an instant read thermometer should read 140 degrees at center). Remove the loin to a cutting board to rest for 20 minutes. Slice into thick medallions and serve with your favorite sides.

6 servings

ORCHARD PEACH ICE CREAM

This ice cream is incredible! At the restaurant, we serve it with little nuggets of almond fried dough.

2 cups milk
1½ cups sugar, divided into 2
6 egg yolks
Pinch of salt
2 cups heavy cream

2 pounds very ripe peaches
Juice of 2 lemons
3 tablespoons vodka
½ teaspoon vanilla extract

Prepare a hot water bath of barely simmering water. Combine the milk with half the sugar and bring to a simmer. Remove from heat. In a bowl that will fit over the water bath, whisk the egg yolks, remaining sugar and pinch of salt. Slowly whisk the hot milk into the egg yolk mixture. Place the bowl over the water bath and stir constantly until the custard thickens and coats the back of a spoon, about 6 minutes. Remove from the heat and immediately add the heavy cream. Strain the mixture into a clean bowl and chill completely. Meanwhile, peel the peaches by plunging them into boiling water for 10 seconds, then immediately into iced water. Slice the peeled and pitted peaches into quarters. Place them in a food processor with the lemon juice and pulse to form a smooth purée. Add the peach purée to the custard, along with the vanilla extract and vodka.

Churn the peach custard in an ice cream machine following manufacturer's directions.

6 servings

EXECUTIVE CHEF TODD MUIR, ST. FRANCIS WINERY

Goat Cheese and Dungeness Crab Pavé
with Smoked Onion Dressing and Roasted Pepper Sauce

Quail Sweet and Sour

Strawberry Martini with Zabaglione

GOAT CHEESE AND DUNGENESS CRAB PAVÉ

Made with garden vegetables and mixed young greens dressed with smoked onion vinaigrette and roasted red pepper sauce.

Pavé is French for the type of paving tiles used in construction. This recipe typifies some of the best of Sonoma County food products including Dungeness crab from the coast, artisan made goat cheese, garden vegetables and mixed young greens. All presented with California Cuisine flare.

Suggested wine: 2000 St. Francis Chardonnay, Sonoma County

6 green zucchini	Salt and pepper
6 yellow zucchini	1 package plain gelatin
3 carrots, peeled	½ cup milk
2 tablespoons olive oil	1 cup chèvre goat cheese
1 teaspoon garlic, minced	1 cup Dungeness crabmeat
1 teaspoon herbes de Provence	

Using a peeler, peel the side of the yellow and green zucchinis, discarding the white seeded center. Stack the slices and cut lengthwise down the middle to make long julienne strips. Slice, stack and julienne the carrots. Blanch the carrots in rapidly boiling water for 1 minute. Heat the olive oil, garlic and herbes de Provence in a large pan. Add the zucchini and carrots. Cook just until the zucchini are limp, about 3 minutes. Season with salt and pepper. Transfer to a large mixing bowl. Sprinkle the gelatin over the milk in a microwavable dish. Mix to dissolve the gelatin. Heat the milk in the microwave for ½ minute on high. Add the goat cheese and crab to the vegetables. Add the milk and mix quickly. Place into a plastic wrap-lined 10 x 3½-inch enamel loaf pan. Gently pack in the pavé mix to eliminate air pockets. Fold the plastic over the top of the pavé, place a weight on top and refrigerate several hours or overnight. Slice and serve with roasted red pepper sauce and mixed young greens tossed with smoked onion vinaigrette.

SMOKED ONION DRESSING

SMOKED ONIONS
1 yellow onion peeled and sliced ¼-inch thick

Using a home-style smoker, place the onion slices on the smoker rack and smoke for about 2 hours. Wrap the smoked onions in aluminum foil and bake in a 350 degree oven for about 45 minutes or until the onions are tender. Chop the smoked onions and refrigerate.

SMOKED ONION VINAIGRETTE

2 tablespoons chopped smoked onions
1 cup extra virgin olive oil

¼ cup red wine vinegar
Salt and pepper to taste

Mix all ingredients together. Season to taste with the salt and pepper.

ROASTED RED PEPPER SAUCE

1 large red bell pepper
2 egg yolks
Juice of 1 lemon
1 cup good olive oil

1 pinch cayenne pepper
1 teaspoon paprika
Salt to taste

Over a gas flame or under a broiler, blacken the pepper all over. Place in a bowl and cover tightly with plastic wrap a few minutes. Under running water, peel the pepper. Remove the seeds and chop. Place the pepper in a blender, add the yolks, lemon and purée. Slowly add the olive oil. Add water if the rouille becomes too thick to add all the oil. Add the cayenne, paprika and season to taste with the salt.

QUAIL SWEET AND SOUR

Elegant and simple, this dish is a real red wine entrée. It is important to find the best balsamic vinegar available. I like to serve these quail with polenta and braised chard.

Suggested wine: 1998 Reserve McCoy Vineyard Cabernet Franc

8 quail semi-boned
Salt and pepper
8 sprigs rosemary
8 slices pancetta

2 tablespoons olive oil
2 tablespoons balsamic vinegar
2 tablespoons honey
¼ cup Zinfandel

Preheat oven to 400 degrees. Season the quail inside and out with salt and pepper. Place a sprig of rosemary in each bird. Wrap the bird with a slice of pancetta and secure with a toothpick. Heat the olive oil in a pan large enough to hold all the quail. Sear the quail a few minutes on all sides. Drizzle each bird with the vinegar and honey. Roast the quail in the oven about 10 minutes. Remove quail from the pan to a serving platter. Deglaze the pan with the wine, scraping any of the little bits in the pan. Pour the sauce over the quail and serve.

4 servings

STRAWBERRY MARTINI
WITH ZABAGLIONE

Strawberries with a splash of red wine syrup topped with zabaglione and crumbled amaretti cookies.

ZABAGLIONE
4 egg yolks   ½ cup Marsala wine
½ cup sugar

Over a double boiler, whisk all ingredients until 3 times its volume, about 8 to 10 minutes. Be careful not to overcook the yolks or they will curdle. You may serve warm as is or you may fold in 1 cup whipped cream and hold, refrigerated for several hours.

TO FINISH
2 cups sliced fresh strawberries   4 amaretti cookies
½ cup red wine syrup

Toss the sliced strawberries with red wine syrup. Divide into 4 martini or margarita glasses. Top with a dollop of zabaglione and one crushed amaretti cookie.

RED WINE SYRUP
2 cups red wine
2 cups sugar

Add the sugar to the wine and boil 10 minutes. Chill well before serving.

4 servings

CHEFS THOMAS ODEN AND FRANCO DUNN, SANTI

A SANTI Autumn Menu

Insalata di Granchio, Finocchio e Cachi

Composed salad of Dungeness crab, shaved fennel,
Fuyu persimmons and Belgian endive with lemon
and extra virgin olive oil

Crespelle di Zucca e Pignoli al Boschetti

Crêpes filled with winter squash and crushed toasted
pine nuts with shallot, white wine and cream sauce topped
with smoked ricotta

Osso Buco di Vitellino SANTI

Petaluma milk-fed veal shanks braised with aromatic vegetables,
sage, rosemary, white wine and tomato sauce with gremolata

Pere Lessate in Vino Rosso ala Crema come Voi

Pears poached in red wine with your choice of
cream accompaniments

INSALATA DI GRANCHIO, FINOCCHIO E CACHI

*Composed salad of Dungeness crab, shaved fennel, Fuyu persimmons
and Belgian endive with lemon and extra virgin olive oil*

6 tablespoons extra virgin
  olive oil
1 tablespoon water

Juice of half a lemon
Salt and pepper

Make the dressing by whisking in the oil, drop by drop, into the
lemon juice and water. Season with salt and pepper.

2 Dungeness crabs, cooked and
  the meat picked, leg meat
  left whole and separate
  from the body meat, or use
  1 pound good quality, fresh
  Dungeness crabmeat

4 Belgian endives, 18 whole
  leaves and the rest sliced
3 persimmons, sliced in rounds
  and cut in half
2 handfuls mixed baby lettuce
1 bunch watercress
2 bulbs fennel, sliced thin

Arrange 3 endive leaves in a three point "star" on each plate. In
between the endive leaves lay down a slice of persimmons. Toss
the baby lettuce, watercress, fennel, sliced endive and body meat
together with the dressing. Place a mound of this mix in the
center of the endive leavers. Arrange the crab leg meat and the
rest of the persimmon slices on top. Season and drizzle with
extra virgin olive oil.

6 servings

CRESPELLE DI ZUCCA
E PIGNOLI AL BOSCHETTI

Crêpes filled with winter squash and crushed toasted pine nuts with shallot, white wine and cream sauce topped with smoked ricotta

FILLING (CAN BE MADE A DAY AHEAD)

2 pounds winter squash (sweetmeat, kabocha or butternut), split and seeded
3 tablespoons toasted pine nuts, coarsely chopped
½ teaspoon chives, chopped fine
Salt and pepper to taste

Bake the squash, cut side down, on a cookie sheet covered with parchment paper at 350 degrees until soft. Flip over to allow trapped steam to escape and cool. Scoop out squash and purée when cool enough to handle. Add other ingredients.

CRÊPES (CAN BE MADE A DAY AHEAD)

2 eggs
Pinch of sea salt
1¼ cups milk, approximately, divided
¾ cup all purpose flour, approximately
3 teaspoons unsalted butter, melted

Mix together eggs, salt and ½ cup milk. Whisk in flour until smooth. Add remaining milk and butter. Allow to rest for 30 minutes. Whisk again, adding a bit of water if the batter needs thinning. Make crêpes in a small non-stick pan over medium heat using a rotating wrist movement and the minimum of batter to just cover the bottom of the pan. When the first side browns on the edges, tap the edge of the pan to loosen the crêpe and flip it over with a spatula or a quick flick of the wrist. After 15 seconds more, remove to a flat surface to cool and repeat until all the batter is used—it should make about 12 crêpes.

SAUCE

1 cup heavy cream
¼ cup dry white wine
1 tablespoon finely chopped shallot
Salt and pepper to taste

Bring to a simmer and remove from heat.

TO SERVE
Grated Parmesan cheese or crumbled smoked ricotta cheese

Place 3 to 4 tablespoons of the filling just off center on each crêpe. Fold in half, then in a quarter circle over the filling. Place the crêpes, with the filled quarter on top, in pairs in a large sauté pan containing half the sauce. Pour the remaining sauce over the crêpes and bring to a boil over high heat. Place in a hot oven until the crêpes begin to brown and the sauce is bubbling. Place a pair of crêpes on each plate and spoon the remaining sauce around them. Sprinkle with grated Parmesan cheese or crumbled smoked ricotta cheese and serve immediately.

6 servings

OSSO BUCO DI VITELLINO SANTI

Sonoma County milk-fed veal shanks braised with aromatic vegetables, sage, rosemary, white wine and tomato sauce with gremolata

6 whole shanks of Sonoma county milk-fed veal, cut into 1¼-inch thick pieces
1 cup unbleached flour
1 tablespoon kosher salt
1 teaspoon black pepper, freshly ground
4 tablespoons extra virgin olive oil (mild flavored)
4 tablespoons unsalted butter
3 sprigs fresh sage
3 sprigs fresh rosemary

6 cloves garlic, papery outer skin removed but thick inner skin left on
1 carrot, small dice
1 stalk celery, small dice
1 small onion, small dice
1 cup dry white wine, at room temperature
1 cup veal stock, at room temperature
1 cup tomato sauce

GREMOLATA
1 lemon, zest only
40 whole parsley leaves

1 garlic clove, sliced paper thin

Warm the shanks to room temperature and dry off any surface moisture with a towel. Mix the flour, salt and pepper together. Heat a large, heavy-bottomed pan that will snugly hold all of the shanks and add half the oil and half the butter to the pan. Dredge the meat in this mixture, carefully shaking off all excess, and place the pieces in the pan of hot oil. Carefully brown each piece on both sides, moderating the heat as necessary to give a nice color without burning the oil. When they are done, move them to a shallow ovenproof roasting pan. Add to the now empty pan the sage, rosemary sprigs, garlic cloves, carrot, celery and onion and allow them to brown a bit in the pan. Then transfer everything to the roasting pan and distribute over the shanks. Tip the pan and remove most of the remaining oil. Add the white wine and cook until reduced by one half. Add the veal stock and the tomato sauce, bring to a boil and pour over the shanks. Cover the shanks with a sheet of parchment paper cut to the size of the pan. Cook slowly in a 325 degree oven until tender (1½ to 2½ hours, usually). Serve each portion with soft or griddle polenta and sprinkle with the gremolata.

6 servings

PERE LESSATE IN VINO ROSSO ALA CREMA COME VOI

Pears poached in red wine with crème anglaise

6 firm pears (best are Bosc, Seckel, Bartlett)
1 bottle red wine
1 cup granulated sugar

1 recipe crème Anglaise, mascarpone crème, whipped cream or vanilla ice cream for topping

Peel the pears and core them from the bottom, saving all of the trimmings. Place the trimmings and the pears in the bottom of a pot that will barely hold them when lying on their side. Cover them with the red wine and the sugar. If the pears are not quite covered with liquid, add a little water to just cover them. Poach the pears until tender over a low flame, turning them gently after 20 minutes. The size and ripeness of the pears will dictate whether the cooking will take 30 or 60 minutes. When done, remove the pears to a shallow dish. Reduce the remaining liquid to a syrup and strain over the pears. Serve warm or at room temperature with some of the syrup and 2 to 3 tablespoons of crème Anglaise, mascarpone crème, whipped cream or vanilla ice cream.

6 servings

Dutchville Creek
Occidental

Coleman Valley Road

J.M. Rosen's Waterfront Grill

In 1996, the opening of J.M. Rosen's Waterfront Grill was hailed as a triumphant return to Petaluma's restaurant scene for sisters Jan and Michele Rosen. Today, that restaurant's success has prompted a second Petaluma restaurant for the gifted pair.

The Rosens started originally in the Great Petaluma Mill in 1976 with the Salad Mill and soon opened a restaurant in Napa. In 1983, they created their renowned cheesecake, made famous by a large list of Hollywood notables who made it a dessert of choice. That cheesecake is now marketed throughout the West Coast and in Washington, D.C.

In 2002, brother Barry Rosen joined Jan and Michele as National and International Director of Sales and Marketing for J.M. Rosen's cheesecake. He is also active in management of Rosen's Eastside Grill.

The dramatic location on the Petaluma River was the lure to attract Jan and Michele back to the Petaluma restaurant scene. "We couldn't pass on that location," Jan said, and a new restaurant was born.

The Rosen's association with Frank Sinatra (a major Rosen's cheesecake aficionado) led to expanding the restaurant in 2001 and opening the Sinatra room for banquets and special occasion. The room features photos and memorabilia of Sinatra and friends.

The restaurant is open Tuesdays through Sundays. Lunch is from 11:30 a.m-2:30 p.m. and dinner is 5:30 p.m.-9:30 p.m. Reservations are advised.

(707) 773-3200

54 East Washington Street

Petaluma, CA 94952

Rosen's Eastside Grill

Following the enormous success of their Petaluma waterfront restaurant, Jan and Michele Rosen set out to open a new restaurant in the Parkway Plaza shopping center on Petaluma's Sonoma Mountain Parkway.

This new restaurant, a popular and critical success, broke different ground for the Rosens. The pair set out to create a neighborhood-style restaurant, with wood paneled booths that evoke elegant eateries from another era.

Shortly after opening in late 2002, the food at Rosen's Eastside Grill was the talk of the town. Although many like to call it "comfort food," the quality ranks with the best.

A wood burning fire produces sought-after rotisserie Rocky the Range Chickens, pizzas, and other house specialties, while each single menu offering is the result of careful planning, research, and application of culinary skills.

The style at Rosen's Eastside Grill is casual, and a single menu suffices for both dinner and lunch. Reservations are not used, and food service is also offered at a full bar.

Jan and Michele Rosen now preside over two of Petaluma's best-loved restaurants, the J.M. Rosen Waterfront Grill, and Rosen's Eastside Grill.

Rosen's Eastside Grill is open seven days a week from 11:30 a.m. until midnight. Cocktails. The kitchen closes at 10:00 p.m.

701 Sonoma Mountain Parkway

Petaluma, CA 94954

763-4644

APPETIZERS

RICOTTA FRITTA ALLA ROMANA

Ricotta Fritters

Chef Maria Belmonte, Caffé Portofino

½ pound ricotta cheese	Vegetable oil
1 cup all purpose flour	½ cup sugar
2 eggs, beaten	Pinch of ground cinnamon

Spread ricotta cheese on a flat plate, making a layer about an inch thick. Cut into 1 by 2 inch pieces. Roll pieces in flour and chill for 1 hour. Roll in flour a second time. Mix with beaten egg. Fry in a large pan with plenty of hot oil. Repeat the process until all pieces are used. When golden brown, drain on a paper napkin and arrange on a serving dish. Sprinkle with a sugar and cinnamon mix. Serve hot.

4 servings

RADICCHIO ALLA GRIGLIA

Grilled Radicchio Stuffed with Goat Cheese

Chef Michael Ghilarducci, The Depot Hotel, Cucina Rustica

8 ounces goat cheese	3 slices pancetta bacon
2 large or 3 small heads radicchio	

Divide and roll the goat cheese into 4 equal cylinders about 3 inches long. Separate the radicchio leaves and wrap 2 to 4 leaves around each cylinder of goat cheese, depending on leaf size. Wrap the pancetta strips around the radicchio bundles and secure with toothpicks as needed. Broil bundles under medium high heat turning frequently to consistently grill all sides. Serve at once, or may be kept warm up to 15 minutes.

4 servings

EGGPLANT ROULADIN

Chef Lisa Hemenway, Lisa Hemenway's Bistro

1 large firm flesh eggplant
Olive oil
2 yellow onions
1 cup diced tomato
2 tablespoons chopped basil

½ cup finely grated Asiago
 cheese
Pinch of allspice
Salt and pepper to taste

Slice eggplant very thin, lengthwise, sprinkle with salt and let rest for 20 minutes. Rinse eggplant, pat dry, rub with olive oil and bake for 5 to 10 minutes.

Slice onions ¼-inch thin and sauté in olive oil until onions begin to brown and caramelize. Add diced tomato and continue cooking until liquids are absorbed. Add chopped basil and Asiago cheese. Season with pinch of allspice, salt and pepper.

Fill and roll eggplant with onion mixture. Serve as an appetizer.

OLIVE SALSA

Chef Jeff Young, Alexander Valley Vineyards

3 tomatoes, peeled, seeded and
 chopped (Brandywine
 tomatoes if available)
1 small sweet onion, minced
4 cloves garlic, minced
¾ cup julienne Hondroelia
 olives or other meaty/mild
 olives

½ cup olives Verte, depitted
 and coarsely chopped
½ cup marinated sun-dried
 tomatoes, julienned
¼ cup AVV Manzinello olive
 oil
Black pepper to taste

Combine all ingredients in a large bowl and let sit for 1 hour before using. I recommend using this salsa for oak-roasted tenderloin of beef.

8 servings

EQUUS CRAB CAKES WITH SPICY RÉMOULADE SAUCE

Executive Chef Doug V. Lane, Equus

A popular gathering place for local residents and business people, as well as travelers, Equus offers a dining experience choreographed by our Executive Chef, Doug V. Lane. The Gallery of Sonoma County Wines, nearly 300 bottles hand picked by their winemakers, sets the tone: wine country splendor in a classic setting.

The Equus Crab Cakes and Spicy Rémoulade Sauce have become essential elements of the restaurant with their Mediterranean touches and textural interplay. They whet the appetite and sate the soul.

CRAB CAKES

1 pound, 4 ounces Dungeness crabmeat (picked through and squeezed dry)
¼ cup chopped celery
¼ cup chopped onion
¼ cup chopped red bell pepper (squeezed dry)
1⅛ teaspoons chopped garlic
3½ teaspoons grated lemon zest
½ teaspoon ground black pepper

2 tablespoons sliced chives
1 egg and 1 egg white
⅓ cup mayonnaise
¼ cup and 2 teaspoons Dijon mustard
⅓-½ cup panko breadcrumbs
1½ ounces additional panko for rolling formed patties in
Olive oil

Combine first 8 ingredients. Bind with next 4 ingredients. Form into small patties (using extra panko) and sear in a nonstick pan with a little olive oil until light brown on one side. Turn cakes over and place pan in 350 degree oven for 5 minutes.

Serve with cabbage slaw or green salad and drizzle with Spicy Rémoulade Sauce.

SPICY RÉMOULADE SAUCE

⅓ cup lemon juice
½ cup chopped yellow onion
½ cup chopped green onions
¼ cup chopped celery
¼ cup prepared horseradish
3 tablespoons whole grain
   mustard
3 tablespoons Dijon mustard
½ cup ketchup
3 tablespoons parsley, chopped
1 teaspoon kosher salt
⅓ teaspoon ground black
   pepper
¾ teaspoon cayenne pepper
¾-1½ cups blend olive oil

Combine all ingredients except olive oil and blend in blender or food processor. Slowly add olive oil while continuing processing/blending. Taste for seasoning.

TERRINE OF FOIE GRAS

Chef Junny Gonzalez, Sonoma Foie Gras

1 pound Sonoma Foie Gras,
   grade "A"
Salt and white pepper
2 tablespoons cognac,
   Armagnac, brandy or white
   wine

Let foie gras set at room temperature for 20 minutes. Remove from package. Cut large and small sections (lobes) apart. Remove visible fat. Cut partially through the bottom of each piece. Open gently with your fingers. Remove and discard large veins. (Muscovy foie gras is really clean, almost no veins.) Sprinkle both sides with salt and pepper. Place in a porcelain terrine smooth side up and press down gently. Sprinkle with the liquor. Cover terrine and refrigerate overnight.

Preheat oven to 200 degrees. Remove foie gras from refrigerator and let set at room temperature for 20 minutes. Place the terrine in a bain-marie, and cook on middle rack of oven for 20 minutes. Remove from oven and let sit covered until cool. The foie gras will have melted somewhat—drain and save the fat for your potatoes. Press foie gras gently back into terrine with upside down lid. Cover and refrigerate for 3 days before serving to enhance the flavor. The terrine can be frozen for several months.

When ready to serve, remove from refrigerator and gently loosen edges with a knife. Remove visible fat and save. Slice foie gras, or serve from the terrine as a spread.

EGGPLANT CAVIAR

Chef Laurie Souza, Korbel Champagne Cellars

1½ pounds eggplant
Olive oil
Salt and black pepper
1 garlic clove, minced

3 tablespoons chopped chives
4 ounces cream cheese
2 Roma tomatoes
10 kalamata olives, chopped

Preheat oven to 400 degrees. Halve the eggplant lengthwise and set cut side up on a baking sheet. Brush surface with olive oil and sprinkle with salt and black pepper. Bake the eggplant until tender, about 35 minutes. Let cool. When cool, scrape the flesh into a strainer and press on the flesh to extract as much liquid as possible. Place eggplant in a food processor. Add the garlic, chives and cream cheese. Process until well mixed. Peel, seed and dice the Roma tomatoes into small dice. Place eggplant in a bowl and stir in the tomatoes and olives. Season with salt and freshly ground black pepper. Cover and refrigerate for at least 2 hours.

Serving suggestions: Pipe onto crackers or cucumber rounds and garnish with fresh chopped chives. Place in a bowl and serve with chips as a dip. Serve on toast with thin slices of onion and quarters of hard-boiled egg.

12 servings

LISA'S DOLMADES

Chef Lisa Hemenway, Lisa Hemenway's Bistro

FILLING

1½ cups couscous or rice
¼ cup currants
¼ cup toasted pine nuts
1 teaspoon thyme
⅛ cup fresh dill
⅛ cup fresh mint

¼ cup sun-dried tomatoes or prosciutto
¼ teaspoon white pepper
½ teaspoon salt
½ tablespoon chopped parsley
2 cups chicken or vegetable stock

Place all ingredients except chicken stock in a large shallow dish. Boil chicken stock and pour over all ingredients (if using rice, cook in chicken stock per directions). Moisten with half the marinade and let rest for 20 minutes.

MARINADE

¾ cup olive oil
¼ cup lemon juice

Zest of 1 lemon
¼ teaspoon cinnamon

Fill grape leaves and place in baking dish. Cover with remaining marinade and bake in 350 degree oven for 35 minutes. Chill and serve with Feta Dip.

FETA DIP

Chef Lisa Hemenway, Lisa Hemenway's Bistro

2 ounces feta cheese
½ cup mayonnaise
½ cup sour cream
1 teaspoon garlic
¼ cup red wine vinegar

1 teaspoon fresh chopped dill and mint
½ tablespoon Worcestershire sauce
Black pepper
Milk to thin

Purée in food processor. Add milk as needed for right thickness.

PESTO

Chef Christine Topolos, Russian River Vineyards

Strip the leaves off the basil, wash them and pack them tightly into a measuring cup. For each cup of basil you will need:

¼ cup pine nuts	1 tablespoon minced garlic
⅓ cup fresh grated cheese	(or more)
½ cup olive oil	Salt and black pepper to taste

Put as much basil in your food processor as it will comfortably hold. Add the ingredients in the order given with the machine running. The coarse texture of the nuts helps to knock the basil roughly around the work bowl so that it doesn't cling to the sides. The protein in the cheese helps to emulsify and incorporate the olive oil. Add the oil in a slow stream.

One cup of basil yields about 1 cup of sauce, enough for a pound of pasta, 4 abundant servings. Pesto freezes very well. Put up in serving sized portions in freezer bags and enjoy the flavor of summer all year round.

We use fresh grated kasseri (a Greek-style sharp cheese) at Russian River Vineyards, but Asiago, Romano or Parmesan will all do well. In any case, a freshly grated cheese will yield a creamier pesto than the pre-grated variety.

Many cookbooks suggest the substitution of walnuts for pine nuts, but then you will lose that resinous smoky undertone. Use pine nuts.

1 cup

Topolos Restaurant - Russian River Vineyards   Freshman '96

EGGPLANT FRITTER

Executive Chef Randy Lewis, Kendall-Jackson Wine Estates, Ltd.

This year at the Sixth Annual Kendall-Jackson Heirloom Festival I came up with the Eggplant Fritter and paired it with a cool glass of fresh heirloom tomato juice. Each September we have the festival featuring hundreds of heirloom tomatoes that we grow at the Kendall-Jackson Wine Center. If you have tomatoes or not, this is just a great, easy hors d'oeuvre.

10 ounces eggplant, peeled
    and cut into strips
Olive oil
2 tablespoons dry Jack cheese,
    shredded

1 egg yolk
1½ tablespoons breadcrumbs
2 mint leaves, chopped
4 basil leaves, chopped
Panko for breading

Simmer eggplant strips for 15 minutes. Strain and sauté eggplant in olive oil for 4 minutes. Cool eggplant. Fold next 5 ingredients into cooled eggplant mixture and form into balls. Bread eggplant balls with panko. Fry in 365 degree olive oil until golden brown. Drain on paper towels and sprinkle with shredded dry Jack cheese.

4 servings

CARAMELIZED APPLE AND TOASTED WALNUT BRIE

Spring Hill Farm

2 tablespoons butter (Spring
    Hill Jersey Cheese Butter)
1 small red apple (such as Fuji
    or Braeburn), cored and
    sliced or chopped
1 tablespoon granulated sugar

1 15-ounce ripe, round Spring
    Hill Jersey Brie Cheese,
    room temperature
¼ cup toasted, coarsely
    chopped walnuts

Melt butter in 10-inch nonstick skillet over medium heat. Add apple slices and sugar. Sauté, tossing occasionally, until apples are soft and golden brown, about 12 minutes. Let apple slices cool slightly. Carefully place chopped apple or fan apple slices over cheese; sprinkle with walnuts. May be served right away or chilled if to be served later. May be prepared several hours in advance. Serve at room temperature. Accompany with assorted crackers and bread slices.

SPRING HILL BREEZE BAKE

Spring Hill Farm

Puff pastry

Spring Hill Jersey Breeze
Cheese

Unroll pastry and wrap the pastry around the Breeze cheese.
Cook it in the oven for 20 minutes at 400 degrees. You can add
any fruit preserve or a pepper jelly to the pastry before you wrap
the cheese for added variety.

GRILLED EGGPLANT
AND SUN-DRIED TOMATO TAPENADE

Chef Robin Lehnhoff, Lake Sonoma Winery

Suggested wine: Valley of the Moon Cabernet Sauvignon

2 large eggplants
½ cup extra virgin olive oil
Salt and pepper to taste
1 large onion, chopped
¼ cup roasted garlic cloves

1 cup sun-dried tomatoes,
   julienned
1-2 tablespoons balsamic
   vinegar
1 anchovy filet, chopped
1 bunch fresh basil

Slice eggplant into ½-inch pieces. Brush with olive oil and
season with salt and pepper. Grill on open flame until cooked
completely. Let cool and cut into large chunks. Combine with
other ingredients in large bowl. In food processor, add tapenade
in batches. Pulse just enough to make a chunky style spread.
Check seasoning with salt and pepper.

VELLA'S CHEESE PUFFS

Sally Vella, Vella Cheese Company

These golden-brown puffs, which resemble cookies, are mouth-watering appetizers or accompaniments for soup or salad. They also freeze well.

2½ tablespoons butter
3½ tablespoons flour
Pinch of salt
Cayenne pepper to taste

5 tablespoons grated Dry Jack cheese
3 egg whites, stiffly beaten

Preheat oven to 400 degrees. Melt butter over medium heat and blend in flour with a whisk. Remove the pan from the heat and blend in salt, cayenne and grated cheese. Fold in egg whites. Drop batter from the tip of a small spoon onto a buttered cookie sheet, leaving 1-inch between spoonfuls. Bake until toasty brown, about 12 to 15 minutes.

About 15 puffs

CLASSIC CEVICHE

Chef Manuel Arjona, Maya Restaurant

It is best to marinate the scallops or snapper in a bowl made of non-reactive materials such as stainless steel, glass or ceramic. The acids may react with other materials, causing discoloration and changes in flavor.

30 ounces fresh red snapper or fresh bay scallops, chopped
1½ cups fresh lime juice
2 cucumbers, finely diced
3 tomatoes, finely diced

2 jalapeño peppers, finely diced
½ cup scallions, chopped
1 cup fresh cilantro, chopped
Salt and pepper to taste
Lime wedges for garnish

In a medium non-reactive bowl, combine seafood with lime juice. Toss to coat thoroughly. Place a sheet of plastic wrap directly on the surface of the seafood to seal completely and refrigerate for 5 hours. While the seafood is marinating, place diced cucumbers into a bowl of salted water and toss well. Let sit for 2 hours, then rinse with cool water and set aside. When the seafood is done marinating, drain well and discard liquid. Return to bowl and toss with remaining ingredients. Add salt and pepper to taste. Garnish with a fresh lime wedge and serve immediately.

8 servings

CRACKER BREAD

Chef Matthew Bousquet, Mirepoix Restaurant

9 pounds all purpose flour
3 tablespoons salt
2 tablespoons sugar
½ pound butter, melted then
  cooled

3 tablespoons yeast
3 cups warm water
  (about 110 degrees)

Combine all dry ingredients. Mix water and yeast, allow yeast to bloom. After butter is cooled, add to liquids. Combine all and knead by hand. Cover and proof until doubles in size. Punch down and roll thin. Brush with oil or butter and top as you wish. We are currently using salt, fresh rosemary (sun-dried and ground in a spice grinder) and red onion. Bake at 375 degrees for about 15 minutes, or until done.

18 servings

BRUSCHETTA

Chef Kathy Young, Lombardi's Gourmet Deli

2 1-pound cans cut tomatoes,
  drained
1 long sour dough baguette
½ cup extra virgin olive oil
9 cloves fresh garlic, peeled
  and sliced thin

1 teaspoon dry Italian
  seasoning
¼ teaspoon kosher salt
¼ teaspoon coarse black pepper
6-8 leaves fresh basil cut in
  pieces

Place drained tomatoes in a medium-sized bowl, set aside. Slice baguette into ½-inch rounds, spread each slice with half the olive oil (lightly). Toast on a cookie sheet, set aside to cool. Add sliced garlic to tomatoes and mix in Italian seasoning, salt and pepper. Spread mixture over the baguette rounds and sprinkle the basil on top. Serve immediately. You can also arrange baguette rounds on a platter and have the bruschetta in a bowl in the center for your guests to serve themselves.

4 to 6 servings

CONFETTI ROUNDS

Chef Kathy Young, Lombardi's Gourmet Deli

3 sour dough French rolls,
   hollowed out
2 8-ounce packages cream
   cheese
¼ pound Italian salami,
   chopped fine
2 cloves garlic, chopped fine

¼ cup chopped parsley
Pinch of coarse pepper
⅛ teaspoon garlic powder
⅛ teaspoon Worcestershire
   sauce
⅛ teaspoon A-1 sauce
1 tablespoon mayonnaise

Blend cream cheese until smooth and add remaining ingredients. Fill each French roll with mixture, packing firmly. Wrap in foil and refrigerate overnight. Slice each roll in ⅛-inch rounds and serve garnished with tomato rosettes and lettuce leaves.

6 to 8 servings

MUSHROOM FRITTATA
WITH SHIITAKE MUSHROOMS

Malcolm Clark, Founder, Gourmet Mushroom, Inc.

¾ cup diced onion
1 clove garlic, minced
8 ounces fresh shiitake
   mushroom
3 tablespoons olive oil
6 eggs
¼ cup breadcrumbs

2 ounces Sonoma Jack cheese
2 tablespoons fresh chopped
   cilantro
½ teaspoon salt
⅛ teaspoon each oregano,
   white pepper, Tabasco
   sauce

If stems of shiitake are tough, remove them and slice caps. Sauté onion, garlic and mushrooms in olive oil over medium heat until barely limp. Beat eggs in large bowl, add the mushrooms and remaining ingredients. Pour into a buttered 7 x 11-inch pan or a round 9-inch pan. Bake in 325 degree oven. Cut into squares or wedges.

6 dozen 1-inch square appetizers
or 6 luncheon-sized wedges

CHEESE AND VEGETABLE APPETIZERS

Patty Karlin, Bodega Goat Cheese

These ideas were presented to the chefs-in-training when the CIA (Culinary Institute of America) toured our ranch on February 5, 2003. The idea is to use cheese to enhance vegetables and move beyond the plain cheese platter or cheese and cracker duo.

RUTABAGAS AND QUESO CABRERO
Peel and slice paper thin rounds of raw rutabagas. Slice paper thin slices of Bodega Goat Cheese Queso Cabrero (manchego style cheese). Top with Saucy Lady or Annie Chu Peanut Cilantro Sauce.

ENDIVES AND QUESO CREMA
Cut endives (red and light green varieties) in half lengthwise. Spread with Bodega Goat Cheese Queso Crema. Then spread with a layer of Marin Gourmet Aubergine (eggplant pesto). Top with finely ground hazelnuts.

PARBOILED GREEN BEANS AND HUANCAINA SAUCE
Parboil green beans (thin, young) in boiling water for 1 minute. Remove and run under cold water to drain and cool. Dip in Huancaina sauce.

HUANCAINA SAUCE
½ teaspoon turmeric
1 jalapeño pepper
10-12 crackers
2 cloves fresh garlic
1 tablespoon olive oil

1 8-ounce container (½ pound) jalapeño or plain goat cheese
Milk to thin to preferred consistency
Salt and pepper to taste

Blend ingredients into a blender

DELICATA SQUASH AND QUESO CABRERO
Halve and seed delicata squash and remove stem. Put upside down in a Pyrex baking dish with water to cover. Cook in 400 degree oven for 20 to 40 minutes until tender. Turn right side up, drain water and put back in oven with grated Queso Cabrero to fill cavity. Remove from oven and top with plum chutney or other chutney.

ABOUT FILO

Robert Engel, Formerly of Topolos' Russian River Vineyards and Restaurant

The following recipe is from the cookbook À La Grecque by Bob Engel and Christine Topolos published by Full Circle Press

A 1-pound package of filo contains about 20 individual leaves. You will find filo in the frozen foods section of most supermarkets. Follow the directions for thawing the filo given on the box. If the dough tears into strips or crumbles as you fold it, it has probably been mistreated in storage; dropped, thawed and refrozen, or otherwise abused. Return it and try a market that might have a higher turnover or take more care with their product.

Many cooks seem intimidated by filo, which is unnecessary. The instructions on the box may warn you to work quickly and keep the dough covered with a damp cloth, but this should be required only on very hot, dry days. If you have your materials assembled and work at a steady pace, you should have no trouble.

Unused portions of the dough can be refrozen, but be very certain to wrap well. Use a plastic freezer bag and seal with freezer tape. Obviously filo which was in poor condition when frozen will not profit from the experience. Save only soft pliable dough.

TIROPITAS - FILO CHEESE TRIANGLES

Robert Engel, Formerly of Topolos' Russian River Vineyards and Restaurant

The following recipe is from the cookbook À la Grecque by Bob Engel and Christine Topolos published by Full Circle Press.

These classic Greek cheese pastries can be made in either appetizer or luncheon size. Three of the luncheon sized triangles make a nice meal. Allow about the same number of the cocktail size per person for hors d'oeuvres.

½ pound feta cheese
¾ cup cottage cheese
1½ tablespoons grated Kasseri
   or Parmesan cheese
1 egg, beaten slightly

2 teaspoons minced parsley
1 dash each of nutmeg and
   white pepper
1 package filo dough
½ pound butter, melted

Place cheeses, egg, parsley, nutmeg and pepper in a bowl and stir with a spoon or fork. Don't mash the bits of feta to a smooth paste. Stir just enough to combine. The luncheon size uses a full sheet of filo folded in thirds.

For the appetizer tiropita, first cut the whole package of filo in thirds. These long strips of filo for the smaller presentation need only be folded in half. Work with one packet at a time. Wrap the extras to protect them from drying out.

Brush a sheet of filo lightly with butter, then fold it in thirds. The technique for folding the triangles is the same, a simple "flag fold". The large tiropita will require a rounded tablespoon of filling; the smaller one just a teaspoon. Brush each strip with butter and fold up. Place on a lightly oiled sheet pan and brush the tops with butter. Bake the hors d'oeuvres size at 375 degrees for 12 to 14 minutes, the large-sized ones for 15 to 20 minutes. The tops should be just golden, not browned deeply. Never microwave filo.

Uncooked tiropitas keep very well. Store in the refrigerator for several days or up to a month in the freezer. Thaw only a few minutes, then bake immediately. Do not store once thawed. These precautions will prevent filo from getting soggy before it has a chance to bake.

20 luncheon sized, 70 or more appetizers

SPICED AHI SEARED RARE WITH WILD MUSHROOMS

Chef Derek McCarthy, Tastings Restaurant and Wine Bar

BALSAMIC GLAZE
2 cups balsamic vinegar
1 thyme sprig
1 rosemary sprig
Mushroom stems

MUSHROOMS
4 tablespoons olive oil
2 tablespoons minced shallots
2 pounds assorted mushrooms
(i.e. shiitake, chanterelle, oyster, cremini) stemmed and sliced
2 tablespoons minced garlic
1 tablespoon chopped fresh thyme
1 tablespoon chopped fresh rosemary
Kosher salt
Black pepper

AHI
1 tablespoon coriander seed
1 tablespoon fennel seed
2 medium bay leaves
2 star anise
1½ pounds ahi tuna, center loin cut (not steak cut)
2 tablespoons kosher salt
1½ tablespoons black pepper
4 tablespoons olive oil

WATERCRESS
Juice of 1 lemon
½ cup extra virgin olive oil
½ pound cleaned and stemmed watercress

For balsamic glaze: Combine balsamic vinegar, mushroom stems, thyme sprig and rosemary sprig in a heavy-bottomed saucepan and bring to a boil. Reduce heat to simmer and continue cooking approximately 8 minutes or until balsamic coats a spoon. Remove from heat, strain and press the herbs and stems. Set glaze aside to cool.

For mushrooms: Sauté mushrooms in 2 batches for better caramelization. Place 2 tablespoons olive oil in largest sauté pan available. Turn heat under pan to high. When pan is hot, add 1 tablespoon of shallots and sauté for 1 minute or until translucent. Add half of the amount of mushrooms, garlic and herbs to sauté pan. Season to taste with salt and pepper. Sauté 5 to 10 minutes on medium high heat until mushrooms are slightly caramelized. Remove from pan and set aside. Repeat procedure with remaining mushrooms, garlic and herbs.

For ahi: Combine spices and grind in a mortar and pestle or spice grinder to form fine powder. Cut ahi into equal rectangular blocks. Coat each piece of ahi with spice powder on all 4 sides and season with salt and pepper to taste. Heat 1 tablespoon olive oil in large sauté pan over medium high heat. When pan is hot, add ahi and sear 1 to 2 minutes on each of all 4 sides (for various temperatures, adjust sear time accordingly). Remove from heat and set aside.

For watercress: Combine lemon juice, olive oil, salt and pepper in mixing bowl. Combine clean watercress with vinaigrette just before serving.

Presentation: Slice ahi into ¼-inch slices. Divide mushrooms into 6 to 8 equal portions and mound in the center of plates. Lean equal portions of ahi slices against the mushrooms. Drizzle balsamic glaze in circle around mushrooms and place seasoned watercress atop mushrooms and serve.

6 to 8 appetizer servings

HAWAIIAN AHI POKE

Chef Ken Tominaga, Hana Restaurant

This recipe is also good for yellowtail, octopus or squid.

3½ ounces sashimi grade tuna per serving
2 tablespoons Poke Sauce
1 tablespoon chopped green onion
1 tablespoon tobiko (flying fish roe)

½ tablespoon toasted white sesame seeds
Chopped pickled ginger (sushi ginger)
Deep fried wonton chips

POKE SAUCE

½ cup soy sauce
¼ cup sesame oil
2 tablespoons extra virgin olive oil

⅓ cup hot chili sauce
2 tablespoons minced garlic

Chop fresh tuna in ¼-inch cubes. Add 2 tablespoons Poke sauce, green onion, tobiko and sesame seed. Mix together. Put on plate in a circle. Garnish with chopped ginger on top of poke. Place deep fried wonton chips around poke.

1 serving

GOAT CHEESE AND WILD MUSHROOM CROSTINI

Chef Phil McGauley, Kenwood Vineyards

1 ounce dried porcini
   mushrooms
1 cup boiling water
2 tablespoons butter
3 cups chopped red onion
3 cloves garlic, minced
1 pound button mushrooms,
   chopped
1 sweet red pepper, chopped
¾ cup Kenwood Sonoma
   County Chardonnay

1½ tablespoons Dijon mustard
1½ tablespoons
   Worcestershire sauce
1½ tablespoons brown sugar
1½ tablespoons soy sauce
1 baguette, cut into 25 slices
7 ounces soft fresh goat cheese
¼ cup pine nuts, toasted
Fresh chopped chives

Pour boiling water over porcini mushrooms and let set for 20 minutes. Strain porcini, saving the liquid. Chop the porcini finely and set aside. In a large sauté pan, melt the butter over high heat. Add onions and garlic, sauté for about 5 minutes. Add porcini mushrooms, button mushrooms and red bell peppers. Sauté until vegetables are tender, about 10 minutes. Add porcini liquid, Chardonnay, mustard, Worcestershire sauce, brown sugar and soy sauce and stir until mixed well. Reduce heat to medium and simmer until most of the liquid has evaporated. Remove from heat and season with salt and pepper. Chill.

Preheat oven to 350 degrees. Arrange baguette slices on a sheet pan and brush lightly with melted butter. Bake until light golden brown. Spread goat cheese evenly on crostini. Spoon 1 tablespoon of mushroom mixture over goat cheese and garnish with pine nuts and chopped chives.

25 crostini

At Clo's range

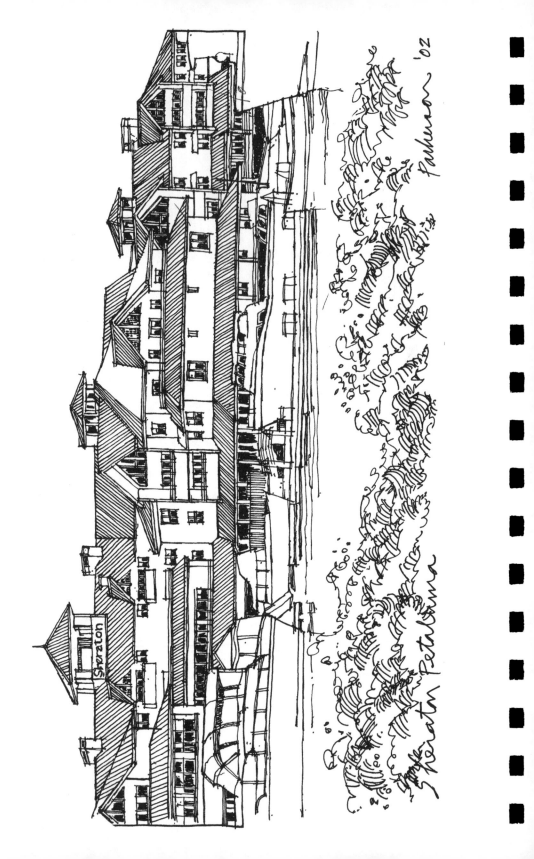

Sheraton

Sheraton Petaluma

Parkinson '02

Sheraton Petaluma Hotel

The 180-room Sheraton Petaluma Hotel, from the outside, has the appearance of the traditional resort hotel. However, the gables and sailboats and park-like setting conceal the fact that behind this attractive facade is one of the most technologically advanced hotels in the world.

The Petaluma hotel, which opened in mid-2002, has attracted attention from the international hospitality industry as the first hotel to install IP Telephony in their guestrooms. The trade magazine Hotels called the Sheraton Petaluma the "leader of the pack", adding that the hotel "adventures into undiscovered territory." Hotel Business magazine lauds them for "pushing the technology envelope".

The purpose of these technical features is to customize and enhance the guest experience. While travelers may scout an area for a hotel that has plug-in and dial-up computer access, the Sheraton Petaluma provides their guests immediate high-speed internet access and programmable speed-dial from the comfort of their room as well as wireless internet access in all public areas and conference rooms.

A next-generation phone system, designed by Cisco Systems, Inc., features a reader display screen, letting the guest pull up information in many areas, from what's on today's restaurant menu to meeting details to stock quotes and flight schedules.

The on-site restaurant, Jellyfish, specializes in naturally raised meats and poultry, seafood from waters off the Sonoma coast and local dairy products and seasonal produce, presented in dramatic dishes inspired by the Far East. Each dish is made to order, not pre-made and stacked to wait, delighting diners with its freshness and creativity.

The Sheraton Hotel is located at the Petaluma Marina on the Petaluma River, at the southern edge of the city. Immediately adjacent to the south is a newly developed wetlands park with walking access featuring a huge array of waterfowl that attracts bird clubs and nature lovers from throughout the North Bay. The entire loop is about four miles.

745 Baywood Drive

Petaluma CA 94954

707-283-2888 FAX 707-283-2828

Armida Winery

A quick turn down Westside Road, a mere three minutes from charming downtown Healdsburg, is the hidden jewel of wine country, Armida Winery. Turn into the driveway and make your way up the curving road past the only traditional aspect of the winery, a lush vineyard of Zinfandel grown in the old-fashioned head-pruned method, allowing the vines to fall to the ground in typical Armida free form fashion.

Continue past the beautiful ponds to the top of the hill where three stunning geodesic domes housing the winery, barrel room and tasting room preside over scenic, sweeping views of the valley below.

Who is Armida Winery? Armida is a consortium of some of the finest minds ever to gather together in a geodesic dome with the purpose of making wine. Coincidentally, we are probably the only minds ever to get together in a geodesic dome with the purpose of making wine. Why geodesic domes?

The practical reasons, according to Buckminster Fuller, would be that the sphere uses the "doing more with less" principle in that it encloses the largest volume of interior space with the least amount of surface area, thus saving on materials and cost.

We at Armida have taken the "doing more with less" philosophy to heart, which is evidenced by what we like to call the "A" team. . . utilizing the largest volume of interior cranial space with the least amount of employee surface area, which translates isnto seven incredible people making 12,000 cases of fantastic wine. We are the Magnificent Seven, a lean, mean, wine-making machine.

And what do we have to show for it? Deep, rich, full-bodied, award-winning wines. Armida is fortunate to receive fruit from three of its finest: the Dry Creek, Russian River and Alexander Valleys. The cooler microclimate of the Russian River Valley provides the perfect setting for our Chardonnay and Pinot Noir grapes, while the warmer growing regions of the Dry Creek and Alexander Valleys produce excellent reds, exemplified in our Zinfandel and Cabernet Sauvignon. These are but some of the fabulous wines we produce . . . all of them great, all of which you should try.

Our tasting room is a beautiful setting in which to taste our wines, many of which are only available at the winery. Bring a picnic, buy a bottle and relax on the deck, overlooking ponds, gardens, vineyards and a great bocce ball court! Experience Armida . . come taste our world.

2201 Westside Road, Healdsburg, CA 95448

707-433-2222   wino@armida.com   www.armida.com
Open for tasting daily

SOUPS

WILD MUSHROOM SOUP

Martin Courtman, Chateau Souverain Café at the Winery

12 tablespoons butter, divided
¾ cup diced onions
¾ cup diced celery
1½ cups potatoes, peeled and diced
1 cup diced leeks (white parts only)
3 whole bay leaves
3 tablespoons freshly chopped parsley stems (no leaves)
1 tablespoon fresh thyme
6 whole garlic cloves, peeled
8 cups vegetable or chicken stock
2 pounds fresh wild mushrooms (gold chanterelles, oyster, shiitake and black trumpet all do well)
2 cups cream
Salt and pepper to taste

Melt 8 tablespoons of the butter in a thick-bottomed saucepan. Add the onions, celery, potatoes and leeks. Cover and cook for a few minutes making sure not to brown them. Add the bay leaves, parsley stems and thyme along with the garlic cloves; stir and cover. Cook at a low heat to sweat all the flavors out of the vegetables and herbs for about 15 minutes, controlling the heat so they do not take on any color. Uncover and let some of the liquid that has formed evaporate (turn the heat up a little to help this along). Pour in the stock, bring to a boil, reduce heat and simmer for 30 minutes.

While the soup base simmers, clean the mushrooms thoroughly and cut to the same size. Season the mushrooms with salt and pepper and sauté in 3 tablespoons butter at high heat until just tender. Place the mushrooms into the soup base after it has cooked about 30 minutes as mentioned. In a separate saucepan, reduce the cream by half by bringing cream to a boil and reducing to a simmer—watch it carefully so it does not scald. Add the cream to the soup and season with salt and pepper. Blend the soup in a blender or food processor and strain through a strainer that is not too fine. Stir in the last tablespoon of butter.

Serve in warmed soup bowls and garnish with either chopped chives or Italian parsley, and a drizzle of white truffle oil.

8 servings

SOUR SHRIMP SOUP (TOM YUM GOONG)

Chef Jiraporn Sujiva, Thai Cuisine

Roasted curry paste can be found in Asian groceries. It is called "num prik pow" in Thai and comes in three flavors, mild, medium and hot. For a vegetarian dish, substitute vegetable and tofu and use thin soy sauce for the fish sauce.

2 pounds medium shrimp
1 cup button mushrooms
6 cups water
1 stalk lemon grass cut into
   2-inch long pieces
3 magrood leaves

1 teaspoon salt
2 tablespoons nampla
   (fish sauce)
3 tablespoons lime juice
1 teaspoon roasted curry paste
Coriander sprigs for garnish

Shell the shrimp except the tail. Remove veins and cut down the center to get the dirt out. Trim the bases of the mushrooms, cut in half, rinse and set aside. Boil water and add the lemon grass and magrood leaves to get the flavor from them. Add shrimp and cook for 3 minutes, then add mushrooms and salt. Remove from heat and season with fish sauce, lime juice and curry paste. Garnish with coriander sprigs and serve.

ROCKIN' MOROCCAN TOMATO SOUP

Executive Chef, Jeffrey Reilly, The Duck Club Restaurant at Bodega Bay Lodge and Spa

2 onions julienne cut
1/4 cup olive oil
2 tablespoons minced garlic
2 tablespoons ground cumin
4 pounds tomatoes, peeled and
   diced
1 cup dry sherry

1/4 teaspoon ground cinnamon
1/2 bunch fresh mint
1/4 teaspoon cayenne pepper
   (or to taste)
1 cup cream (optional)
Salt and pepper

Sauté onions in olive oil on medium heat until lightly caramelized. Add garlic and cumin and cook for 1 minute. Add sherry and reduce by half. Add tomatoes and simmer for 5 minutes. Purée in blender until smooth. Add cinnamon, mint, cayenne and cream. Season with salt and pepper. Serve warm.

4 to 6 servings

ROASTED PEAR
AND BUTTERNUT SQUASH SOUP

Chef Tai Oleski, Hilton Hotel

2 medium butternut squash, halved and seeded
4 Bosc pears, peeled, quartered and seeded
⅓ cup olive oil
1 teaspoon white pepper
2 teaspoons cinnamon, divided
2 teaspoons curry powder, divided
2 teaspoons kosher salt, divided
5 tablespoons butter
3 cups diced white onion
1 cup diced celery (inner lighter colored stalks with leaves on)
4 cups chicken stock
2 cups heavy cream
½ cup toasted pumpkin seeds
¾ cup sour cream

Place squash and pears in a large mixing bowl. Add the olive oil, pepper and 1 teaspoon each of the cinnamon, curry powder and salt. Toss until evenly coated. Place the squash and pears on a roasting rack or oiled sheet pan and cook at 375 degrees until golden brown and tender to the touch (approximately 30 minutes for the pears and 10 minutes longer for the squash). After cooling slightly, scrape the flesh from the skin of the squash and reserve on the side with the pears.

In a saucepan melt the butter. Add onions and celery and sauté over medium heat until soft and translucent (about 8 minutes). Add the remaining cinnamon, curry powder and salt to the onion and sauté another minute. Add the squash, pears and stock. Put in blender or food processor and blend until smooth. Return back to saucepan, add cream and bring to a boil.

Spoon into bowls and top with a dollop of sour cream and a few of the pumpkin seeds.

10 to 12 servings

CREAM OF CARROT SOUP

Chef Joseph, Joseph's Restaurant and Bar

6 medium carrots, 3 chopped
and 3 shredded
2 stalks celery
¼ small leek
1 medium potato
1 medium onion, chopped
½ cup rice
1 pint heavy cream

1 pint milk
2 ounces butter
2½ quarts chicken stock
2 tablespoons parsley, chopped
Salt, pepper, soy sauce,
Worcestershire sauce to
taste
Parsley for garnish

Chop 3 carrots, the celery, leek and potato into chunks. Cook onions in butter until just translucent. Add chopped vegetables and rice. Stir over medium heat for 3 to 4 minutes. Add stock to vegetables and simmer for 30 to 45 minutes. Purée cooked mixture. Add cream, milk and shredded carrots. Bring just to boiling point and reduce heat. Season to taste with seasonings. Allow to simmer for 5 to 10 minutes. Garnish with parsley.

10 to 12 servings

SWEET CORN AND SCALLOP BISQUE

Chef Jean-Claude Balek, Bay View Restaurant and Lounge, The Inn at the Tides

3 tablespoons extra virgin
olive oil
2 medium red onions, medium
dice
1 pound fresh scallops,
cleaned, medium dice
1 bottle (750 ml) dry white wine

1 gallon fish stock
1 gallon chicken stock
10 ears sweet corn, husked
1 pound fresh tarragon
½ gallon heavy cream
Salt and black pepper

In soup pot, heat the olive oil and sweat the onions until translucent. Add the scallops and wine. Reduce the wine by half. Add the fish stock and again reduce by half. Then add the chicken stock and reduce by half. With a box grater, grate the corn directly into the pot. Add the tarragon and cream. Simmer for 15 to 20 minutes. Then purée the soup with an emulsion blender or a bar blender. Strain through a medium sieve and season to taste with salt and pepper. Tarragon sprigs and a good quality olive oil drizzle make up the garnish.

8 4-ounce servings

GRAVENSTEIN APPLE GAZPACHO

Carol Kozlowski-Every, Kozlowski Farms

Apples in gazpacho are a secret ingredient of Spain

6 large ripe tomatoes, skins removed

1 large English cucumber, peeled, seeded and coarsely chopped

1 green bell pepper, seeded, peeled and quartered

1 red bell pepper, seeded, peeled and quartered

1 small red onion, quartered

1 clove garlic, smashed

2 Gravenstein apples, peeled and quartered

Juice of 1 lemon

1 cup fresh French bread, crust removed, cubed

3 tablespoons Kozlowski Farms Red Raspberry Vinegar

¼ cup extra virgin olive oil

4 cups chilled tomato juice

¼ teaspoon Tabasco sauce (or more if you prefer a bite to your gazpacho!)

Salt and pepper to taste

Extra French bread cubes for crouton garnish

In food processor, liquefy tomatoes. Set aside in large bowl. Working with 1 ingredient at a time, continue processing cucumbers, green and red bell peppers, onion, garlic, apples and lemon juice until smooth. Soak 1 cup of French bread cubes in Red Raspberry Vinegar and olive oil. Liquify. Stir all ingredients together in large bowl. Add chilled tomato juice until you reach a desired soup-like consistency. Season with salt and freshly ground pepper to taste. Add Tabasco sauce to taste. Chill well. Garnish with toasted French bread cubed before serving.

Other Gazpacho garnish: Chopped tomatoes, chopped onions, chopped cucumber, chopped bell peppers, chopped avocado tossed in lemon juice, chopped cilantro.

6 to 8 servings

CHILLED SONOMA
TOMATO-VEGETABLE SOUP

Martin Courtman, Executive Chef, Chateau Souverain Café at the Winery

16 ripe tomatoes, blanched,
  peeled and seeded
4 English cucumbers, peeled
  and seeded
4 red bell peppers, peeled and
  seeded
2 celery stalks
½ medium onion
1 jalapeño pepper, cored,
  seeded and chopped fine

1 serrano chile, cored, seeded
  and chopped fine
2 ounces sherry wine vinegar
8 ounces tomato juice
3 ounces olive oil
¼ cup chopped mixed herbs
  (Italian parsley, chives,
  cilantro and tarragon)
Salt, freshly ground pepper
  and cayenne pepper to taste

After vegetables have been peeled, cored and seeded, cut everything into 1-inch pieces. Place them in a stainless steel bowl along with the jalapeño pepper and serrano chile. Add the vinegar, tomato juice and olive oil. Season lightly with salt, freshly ground pepper and cayenne pepper. Cover tightly and refrigerate overnight, stirring occasionally. Place mixture in a food processor and, using the pulse setting, mince until the vegetables are fine but still have some texture to them. Return mixture to bowl and add the freshly chopped herbs. Correct the seasoning (to taste). Chill well and serve in ice cold bowls.

12 servings

FRESH PUMPKIN-GINGER SOUP

Chef Robin Lehnhoff, Lake Sonoma Winery

Suggested wine: Lake Sonoma Chardonnay

2 cups chopped yellow onion
1 cup chopped celery
1 cup peeled and chopped
    carrot
1 1-inch piece fresh ginger
1 medium sugar pumpkin
    (peeled, seeded and
    chopped into 1-inch
    chunks)

4 tablespoons butter or olive
    oil
1 cup Lake Sonoma
    Chardonnay
8 cups chicken or vegetable
    stock
2 teaspoons kosher salt
½ teaspoon cayenne pepper
Crème fraîche and toasted
    almonds for garnish

Sauté onion, celery, carrot, ginger and pumpkin in butter until they sweat. Add wine and cook 10 minutes. Add stock, salt and cayenne pepper. Bring soup to a boil and then reduce heat and let simmer for 30 to 45 minutes. Remove from heat and let cool slightly. Purée in blender until nice and smooth. Re-season with salt and pepper if necessary. Garnish with crème fraîche and toasted almonds.

8 to 10 servings

SIMPLE GARDEN TOMATO SOUP

Chef Jesse Mallgren, Madrona Manor

1 medium yellow onion, sliced
    thin
2 peeled cloves garlic
¼ cup extra virgin olive oil

2 pounds heirloom tomatoes,
    rough chopped
¼ cup fresh whole basil leaves
Salt and pepper to taste

Sweat onions and garlic in the olive oil on low heat until both are soft (about 20 minutes), making sure they do not burn. Add tomatoes and continue cooking for another 20 minutes or until all of the large chunks of tomato are soft. Turn off heat and add basil to the pot. Let sit for 30 minutes. Pass soup through a fine meshed food mill. Next, strain through a fine meshed strainer. Season to taste. Heat and serve with your favorite bread.

4 servings

TURKISH RED LENTIL SOUP WITH PRESERVED LEMON

Chef Robin Lehnhoff, Lake Sonoma Winery

2 tablespoons olive oil
1 large onion, chopped
1 tablespoon ground coriander
2 teaspoons ground cumin
1 teaspoon ground ginger
2 tablespoons Dijon mustard
1 pound dry red lentils

1 preserved lemon, julienned
10 cups water or stock
Salt and pepper to taste
1 cup plain yogurt
¼ cup fresh cilantro, minced
Juice of 1 lemon

Sauté onion, spices and mustard in oil until slightly browned. Add lentils, preserved lemon with stock and bring to boil. Reduce heat and simmer for 15 minutes. Season with salt and pepper. Combine yogurt, cilantro and lemon juice. Drizzle over soup as a garnish.

8 to 10 servings

PAPPA AL POMODORO

Tomato Bread Soup

Chef Dennis, Cucina Paradiso Ristorante Italiano

3 large cloves garlic
½ cup olive oil
Pinch of crushed red pepper
1 pound very ripe tomatoes
   (fresh or canned)

1 pound Tuscany bread
3 cups hot chicken or meat
   broth
Salt and fresh ground black
   pepper
4-5 leaves basil

Chop the garlic coarsely, then place in a stock pot with olive oil and crushed red pepper. Sauté for 10 minutes. Cut and blend the tomatoes (remove the seeds) and add to the pot. Simmer for 15 minutes. Cut the bread in cubes, toast in oven until golden and then add to the pot. Add broth, salt, pepper and basil. Simmer for 15 more minutes and remove from heat.

To serve: Add 1 tablespoon of olive oil, fresh basil and ground pepper.

4 servings

LOBSTER SOUP

Chef Matthew Bousquet, Mirepoix Restaurant

4 cups lobster stock,
   recipe follows
1 cup heavy cream
4 tablespoons butter

4 tablespoons flour
2 tablespoons lemon juice
Salt and pepper to taste

Place lobster stock in a heavy-bottomed pot and reduce by 25 percent to concentrate flavor. In a separate pan, make a roux by melting the butter and stirring in the flour. Allow to cook for 4 to 5 minutes to let the flour cook. Remove ½ of the roux and save (blond roux). Place the other half in the oven at 350 degrees until dark brown (dark roux). Remove and allow to cool. After lobster stock has reduced, add cream and reduce by 25 percent. Add both roux while stirring. Roux is a thickener that is activated in boiling liquid. If too thick, add more cream. If too thin, add more blond roux. Season with salt and pepper and add lemon juice. Serve hot.

8 servings

LOBSTER STOCK

Chef Matthew Bousquet, Mirepoix Restaurant

4 lobster shells and bodies
   (gills and entrails removed)
1 tablespoon canola oil
½ pound mirepoix—chopped
   and peeled carrot, onion,
   leek, fennel, 2 cloves garlic
2 tablespoons tomato paste

½ cup brandy
1 cup dry white wine
1 vanilla bean (optional)
4 cups water
1 bouquet garni—pinch of
   parsley, pinch of thyme,
   peppercorns, bay leaves

Place lobster shells in a heavy-bottomed pot with canola oil and roast very slowly until shells turn bright red. Add mirepoix and caramelize, about 15 to 20 minutes. Add tomato paste and cook an additional 5 to 7 minutes. Add brandy, watch for the flaming of the brandy—you may want to remove the pan from the flame as you do this. Cook over a low flame until liquid is reduced by 80 percent. Add white wine and reduce by half. Add water, vanilla bean and bouquet garni, then simmer for about 1 hour. Strain. Refrigerate, will last up to 5 days.

4 cups

POTATO AND LEEK SOUP WITH TRUMPET ROYALE™

Chef Bob Engel, Gourmet Mushrooms, Inc.

Gourmet Mushrooms, Inc. is dedicated to sustainable farming in Sonoma County and across North America. The company is a pioneer in growing exotic culinary mushrooms and helps others to establish farms using the same method. These delicious mushrooms are grown on a medium composed primarily of oak shavings left over from wine barrel manufacture. Growing mushrooms on this material gets a second use out of a by-product that would otherwise be wasted. After harvesting the mushrooms, the spent medium is composted and returned to the land. This is a model for low-impact craft farming that contributes to the economic and nutritional health of the area, while having a positive effect on the environment...and our menus.

½ cup diced onion
3 tablespoons butter
1 pound russett or Yukon gold potatoes, peeled and roughly diced
2 medium leeks, white part only, halved, sliced and washed
2 stalks celery, chopped
1 bay leaf

Water sufficient to cover, about 3 cups
½ cup cream or half-and-half, more to taste
½ pound Trumpet Royale™ mushrooms, sliced
1 clove garlic, minced
2 tablespoons olive oil
2 tablespoons dry sherry
Salt and pepper to taste

Sauté onion in the butter in a 3 or 4-quart saucepan over medium heat until the onion begins to turn translucent. Add the potato, leek and celery. Continue cooking about 5 minutes. Do not let vegetables brown. Add bay leaf and sufficient water to just cover the vegetables. Simmer until potatoes are very soft. Remove bay leaf, then purée in food mill or food processor. (For food processor, use pulse, do not overwork.) Return the mixture to the saucepan and add cream and/or milk or water to desired consistency. Keep warm.

Meanwhile, sauté the mushrooms and garlic in the olive oil until cooked through, about 5 minutes. Stir mushrooms into the soup. Deglaze the mushroom skillet with the sherry and add this to the soup. Add salt and pepper to taste.

4 servings

TOM KHA (COCONUT SOUP)

Chef Thanit, Pad Thai Restaurant

2¼ cups coconut milk
2 tablespoons fish sauce
2 tablespoons lemon juice
1 tablespoon sugar
1 tablespoon chili paste with
   soybean oil
½ cup mushrooms
½ cup sliced chicken

¼ cup sliced yellow onion
5 pieces sliced lemon grass
5 pieces sliced galanga
5 pieces kaffir lime leaves
1 tablespoon chopped cilantro
1 tablespoon chopped green
   onions

Boil coconut milk over medium heat with lemon grass, galanga and lime leaves for 5 minutes. Add fish sauce, lemon juice, sugar, chili paste and chicken. Boil until chicken is cooked. Remove from heat. Add mushrooms, green onions and cilantro before serving.

Notes: Galanga is a root similar to ginger but with different color and flavor. It is milder than ginger and usually white. Fish sauce comes in a bottle like soy sauce and is not hard to find. All the other ingredients can be found in local Sonoma County Asian markets.

Jerico . . .
The Hidden Secret of the
Best of Sonoma County

From the terraced hillside vineyards to the verdant dairy land that hugs the Sonoma coast, Jerico Products, Inc. plays an integral role in bringing the best of Sonoma County to your table.

You may not know it, but the best wine, dairy products, produce, chicken and eggs produced in Sonoma County have been touched by Jerico. When you sip a gold medal winning chardonnay, Jerico's Pacific Pearl Oyster Shell Flour was used to lime the vineyards, providing the essential calcium for optimum growth and plant health. Your favorite fresh, locally grown fruits and vegetables flourish in soil amended with Pacific Pearl Oyster Shell Flour.

Wholesome, versatile Clover dairy products are produced by cows who benefit from the calcium boost provided by Pacific Pearl products, and even your Sunday-best frittata or Eggs Benedict recipe is enhanced by local eggs - which had a greater chance of making it to the market with healthier chickens and stronger eggshells as a result of adding Pacific Pearl Lay Blend to the hen's feed.

You may not know Jerico Products, Inc. by name, but when you add up all the local restaurants, bakeries, caterers and home chefs cooking with Sonoma County products, it's clear that Jerico contributes to the quality of life that makes Sonoma County a true gourmet paradise.

100 East "D" Street
Petaluma, CA 94952
707-762-7251 - 707-762-2129

G&G Supermarkets
Santa Rosa and Petaluma

G&G Supermarket has supplied quality groceries to Sonoma County residents since1963. G&G opened its second location in November of 2000 on Sonoma Mountain Parkway in Petaluma.

Independently owned and operated by the Gong family, G&G features a wide variety of gourmet and regular grocery items. Both stores feature a large delicatessen department, a fresh fish and meat department, fresh floral department, large produce department with a wide variety of fresh vegetables and fruits, and an in-store bakery.

There is also a wide selection of wines and liquors, a take-out hot delicatessen with prepared Chinese food and fried chicken, an in-store sushi chef, and much more.

The Santa Rosa store is the largest independent grocery store in Northern California, measuring more than 93,000 square feet. A large Asian and Hispanic food section is included.

The bakery has ready-made cakes, desserts, donuts, breads, special-order cakes and wedding cakes.

G&G's floral designers arrange beautiful arrangements for weddings, birthdays, anniversaries and other special occasions. Green and flowering plants, orchids, azaleas, gift baskets and more are also for sale.

The deli features more than 80 different types of gourmet deli meats such as prosciutto, ham, westphalian ham, mortadella, pâté and more. The gourmet cheese island features more than 60 different types of domestic and European cheeses, such as gorgonzola, blue cheese, fontina, gouda, French brie, teleme, and marscapone.

The old-fashioned meat and fresh seafood department features prime cuts of aged beef cut to your specifications. Fresh seafood, lobster, salmon, prawns and a wide selection of local fish are also available.

Visit us and see first-hand why G&G has been a favorite shopping destination for more than 35 years! We are happy to be a part of the Sonoma County community, and proud to be a supporter of a broad range of community efforts.

1211 W. College Ave	701 Sonoma Mountain Parkway
Santa Rosa, CA	Petaluma, CA
707-546-6877	707-765-1198

Hilton Sonoma County/Santa Rosa

Nestled in the heart of Sonoma County wine country, the Hilton features breathtaking views of the Santa Rosa valley. Situated on 13 acres of beautifully landscaped grounds, the chalet style hotel offers beautifully appointed rooms and amenities.

Our Harvest Grill restaurant features an eclectic blend of "Sonoma Fresh" cuisine prepared by Executive Chef Tai Olesky. Offering exquisite views, the patio is the perfect place to sample award-winning local wines.

The Hilton Sonoma County/Santa Rosa is located near 140 world-class wineries, championship golf courses, the Armstrong Woods, and the scenic Russian River and Sonoma Coast. For reservations call (800) HILTONS or (707) 523-7555

3555 Round Barn Boulevard

Santa Rosa CA 95403

www.winecountryhilton.com

Bodega Goat Cheese

is a distinctive Peruvian style Goat Cheese, 100% whole pasteurized goat milk, herbs and sea salt with no animal rennet or additives.

Each step in the cheese's production, from pasture to market, insures freshness, full flavor and a unique, natural, handcrafted product. The fastidious adherence to quality production responds to the rigorous demands of California gourmet shoppers who want to know where their food originated, and how it is made. Our present permaculture project is the consumer's assurance of quality as we move toward 100% sustainable, organic agriculture.

Ask us about our licensing/apprentice program.

This versatile goat cheese is adaptable to any recipe calling for a stuffing cheese, a melting cheese or a cream cheese.

Javier Salmon/Patty Karlin
P.O. Box 223
Bodega, CA 94922
Phone and Fax 876-3483
e-mail bdgagoat@sonic.net

Richard's Stone and Saralee's Vineyard – Windsor

Parkearn '96

SALADS

WARM SHRIMP SALAD
WITH GRILLED PINEAPPLE SALSA

Chef Phil McGauley, Kenwood Vineyards

DRESSING

1 clove garlic, minced
1 shallot, minced
1 tablespoon fresh cilantro, chopped
1 teaspoon fresh ginger, grated
2 tablespoons lime juice
1½ tablespoons rice wine vinegar
1½ teaspoons soy sauce
¼ cup olive oil
1 teaspoon sesame oil
Salt and pepper to taste

Combine all the dressing ingredients in a food processor and mix until well blended. Season with salt and pepper. Set aside.

SALAD

16 large prawns, peeled and deveined
3 cups spring mix lettuce
1 cup arugula
½ cup diced sweet red pepper
½ cup diced sweet yellow pepper
Chopped chives
Grilled Pineapple Salsa (recipe to follow)

Marinate prawns in 3 tablespoons of dressing for about 20 minutes. Grill the prawns over a hot grill until translucent. Pour enough dressing over the lettuce just to coat. Arrange the lettuce on 4 plates with about ¼ cup of pineapple salsa in the middle. Place 4 prawns around the salsa with a scatter of red and yellow bell pepper. Garnish with chopped chives and dressing on the side.

4 servings

GRILLED PINEAPPLE SALSA

Chef Phil McGauley, Kenwood Vineyards

1½ cups pineapple, grilled and cut into ½-inch pieces
¼ cup firm tomatoes, seeded and diced
¼ cup diced mango
1 teaspoon serrano chili, seeded and diced
¼ cup diced red onion

1½ tablespoons rice wine vinegar
½ teaspoon honey
1 tablespoon fresh lime juice
½ teaspoon ground cumin
2 tablespoons chopped fresh cilantro leaves
Salt and pepper to taste

Mix all ingredients together gently so they retain their shape. Season with salt and pepper. Keep at room temperature.

SPRING HILL JERSEY SALAD

Spring Hill Farm

3 Belgian endive, cut into ½-inch rings
3 cups fresh baby spinach
2 Granny Smith apples, sliced into ⅛-inch thick wedges
2 teaspoons chopped basil

¼ cup extra virgin olive oil
¼ cup apple cider vinegar
Salt and freshly ground pepper to taste
1 cup Spring Hill horseradish Quark Cheese

Wash spinach and endive, pat dry, place in a large bowl and toss gently. Add apple wedges and basil to bowl and toss gently. Mix olive oil and vinegar in separate bowl. Add salt and pepper to taste. Splash on salad until all ingredients are lightly coated. Salad can be served in one large bowl or individually plated. The last step is to sprinkle the salad with dime-sized pieces of quark cheese.

4 to 6 servings

BABY SPINACH SALAD WITH WARM SONOMA GOAT CHEESE

Executive Chef, Jeffrey Reilly, The Duck Club Restaurant at Bodega Bay Lodge and Spa

FOR GOAT CHEESECAKES

1 egg with ¼ cup water, mixed well for egg wash
6 2-ounce medallions goat cheese

1 cup panko, toasted
½ cup ground toasted almonds
½ bunch chives, finely cut

Form 2-ounce medallions of cheese and put into egg wash. Roll in almond and chive breading. Place in 350 degree oven for 8 minutes to warm.

ORANGE SHERRY VINAIGRETTE

¾ cup pure olive oil
⅓ cup aged sherry vinegar
¼ cup orange juice concentrate

2 shallots, finely diced
3 tablespoons fresh tarragon, chopped
Salt and pepper to taste

Blend all ingredients together.

OTHER SALAD INGREDIENTS

9 cups clean baby spinach
3 oranges, peeled and cut into segments
½ cup sliced blanched almonds, lightly toasted

¾ cup tart, dried Michigan cherries, soaked in 1 cup port wine, heated on low heat until cherries absorb all the port

SALAD ASSEMBLY

Toss spinach in vinaigrette. Top with oranges, cherries and almonds. Put warm goat cheese medallions on top and you're in luck, you've made one sweet salad.

6 servings

TOMATO TAPENADE CAESAR SALAD

¾ cup mayonnaise
Juice of 1 lemon
¼ cup red wine vinegar
4 teaspoons grated Parmesan
  cheese
3 teaspoons anchovy paste
  (or to taste)
1 teaspoon sugar

1 teaspoon dry mustard
2 teaspoons dried tomato
  tapenade
1 teaspoon Worcestershire
  sauce
1 teaspoon coarse ground
  pepper

Combine ingredients in a bowl and whisk to combine thoroughly. Refrigerate to marry flavors. Serve over torn romaine lettuce.

GREEK SALAD

Robert Engel, Formerly of Topolos' Russian River Vineyards and Restaurant

The following recipe is from the cookbook À la Grecque by Bob Engel and Christine Topolos published by Full Circle Press.

A true Greek salad contains no lettuce. The base is wedges of tomato and sliced cucumber, accented by crumbled feta cheese, thinly sliced red onion, parsley and kalamata olives. But all these are nothing if the dressing isn't just right. This recipe is a surprisingly simple one that will only be as good as the ingredients used. A good Greek olive oil, slightly green and fruity, real Greek oregano and a strong varietal red wine vinegar are essential.

1¾ cups Greek olive oil
½ cup red wine vinegar
1 tablespoon Greek oregano

1 teaspoon salt
1 pinch each of dill, thyme
  and mint

Whisk all together in a bowl or shake in a jar to blend.

Assemble the salad in layers with tomatoes and cucumbers on the bottom, then the feta, red onions and parsley in that order. Garnish with olives and Greek pepperoncini. Drizzle the dressing generously over the top just before serving. There should be dressing to spare in which to dip the bread.

2½ cups dressing

BUTTER LETTUCE SALAD

with Fresh Artichoke Hearts and Tarragon

Michele Anna Jordan

Butter lettuce is the most delicate of all salad greens and is a perfect canvas for the flavors of fines herbes.

4 jumbo artichokes, boiled until tender, drained and cooled
2 tablespoons butter
4 teaspoons minced fresh tarragon divided
2 teaspoons minced fresh Italian parsley
2 teaspoons fresh snipped chives

2 teaspoons minced fresh chervil
1 head butter lettuce, leaves separated
Kosher salt
Extra virgin olive oil
Champagne or white wine vinegar or ½ lemon
4 small tarragon sprigs

Remove all of the artichoke leaves and set them aside for another use. Remove and discard the choke and trim the heart. Melt the butter in a small pan, add 2 teaspoons of the tarragon, set aside and keep warm.

In a small bowl, toss together the remaining 2 teaspoons fresh tarragon, the parsley, the chives and the chervil.

Put the butter lettuce in a large bowl, sprinkle lightly with kosher salt and toss gently. Drizzle a tablespoon or 2 of olive oil over the greens, toss, drizzle with 2 teaspoons or so of vinegar or lemon juice and toss again. Add the sliced avocado, scatter the herb mixture on top and toss gently.

Divide the greens among 4 individual plates. Set an artichoke heart on each plate. Heat the butter-tarragon mixture until it is very hot and spoon some over each artichoke heart. Add 2 crackers to each plate, garnish with a tarragon sprig and serve immediately.

4 servings

AHI TUNA SALAD

Pacific Connection Catering for Rodney Strong Vineyards

Suggested wine: Reserve Pinot Noir

4 yellow beets
4 red beets
1 pound new potatoes
Olive oil
Salt and pepper to taste
3 red bell peppers
1 pound French green beans

½ cup hazelnut oil
6 tablespoons balsamic vinegar
½ cup beet juice reduced to
    ¼ cup
8 6-ounce ahi tuna filets
8 small heads butter lettuce

Cook the beets (skins included) in a 400 degree oven for about 45 minutes until they are done. When cool, peel and quarter. Keep the red beets separate so they will not bleed all over. Set aside. Cut new potatoes in half and sprinkle with olive oil and salt and pepper. Roast in the oven until they are done. Roast the red peppers on open flame or burner until blackened. Remove skins. Cut into ¼-inch slices and set aside. Blanch beans until they are cooked (approximately 2 minutes in boiling water). Cool in an ice bath and set aside. Combine the oil with the vinegar, beet juice and salt and pepper. Season the tuna with salt and pepper and grill until medium rare and set aside.

Wash the butter lettuce and lay on plates. Arrange the vegetables and tuna on the lettuce and drizzle with the vinaigrette.

8 servings

SONOMA SUMMER SALAD WITH GRILLED TUNA

Martin Courtman, Executive Chef, Chateau Souverain Café at the Winery

Please read all directions first.

MARINADE

4 tuna steaks, 5 ounces each (approximately 1-inch thick)
2 teaspoons anchovy purée
2 teaspoons chopped fresh tarragon
2 teaspoons chopped Italian parsley
2 tablespoons chopped shallots
1 tablespoon fresh lime juice
1 cup olive oil
½ teaspoon Tabasco sauce

Mix all ingredients together. Place tuna steaks in the marinade and chill in refrigerator for 1 hour prior to grilling.

FOR THE SALAD

8-12 ounces spring mix (depending on the desired size of the salad)
24 sugar snap peas, blanched
½ small cucumber, peeled, seeded and diced
4 ounces Grain Mustard Vinaigrette (may vary to your preference)
Salt and freshly ground pepper
2 hard-boiled eggs, cut into fourths
4 Roma tomatoes, peeled and cut into fourths
1 avocado, peeled and sliced
12 black olives

In a large bowl, place the spring mix, snap peas, cucumbers and vinaigrette. Season with salt and pepper. Continue to toss the salad lightly until well mixed. Divide evenly onto 4 plates and add the egg, tomato, avocado and olive.

GRAIN MUSTARD VINAIGRETTE

12 ounces Chateau Souverain Chardonnay (reduce slowly to 4 ounces)
2 teaspoons whole grain mustard
2 cups canola oil
1 teaspoon chopped shallots
1 teaspoon chopped fresh tarragon
Salt and freshly ground pepper to taste

Place the 4 ounces of reduced Chardonnay in a blender with the mustard. Blend on slow for 30 seconds and then add the oil very slowly. Once emulsified and all the oil has been added, turn off the blender and pour into a small bowl. Add the shallots and tarragon. Season with salt and pepper. Refrigerate unused vinaigrette for up to 1 week. Shake or place in blender as it separates.

2½ cups

THE FINAL PRODUCT
When ready to serve the Sonoma Summer Salad, it is important that everything is timed right. As soon as the tuna has marinated for about 1 hour, remove each steak and place on a hot grill. For a medium-rare finish, grill tuna for 3 to 4 minutes on each side. Season with salt and freshly ground pepper just before placed on the freshly tossed salad. Serve immediately sprinkled with edible flower petals for a beautiful touch.

1 serving per tuna steak

Estero Americano

GREEN PAPAYA SALAD

Chef Thanit, Pad Thai Restaurant

1 cup shredded green papaya	1 tablespoon lemon juice
¼ cup shredded carrot	1 tablespoon fish sauce
3 pieces raw string beans	1 tablespoon sugar
1 medium-sized tomato	¼ head iceberg lettuce or
¼ cup roasted peanuts, mashed	green cabbage

Put shredded green papaya and carrots in a mixing bowl. Cut off the ends of raw string beans and chop and mash beans and pods together. Cut the tomato into 5 pieces. Add tomato wedges, mashed peanuts and beans to papaya and carrots. Toss salad with lemon juice, fish sauce and sugar. Serve on a bed of crisp iceberg lettuce or green cabbage leaves.

ARTICHOKE SALAD

with Vella Mezzo Secco Jack Cheese
in Meyer Lemon Dressing

Chef Carlo Cavallo, Meritage Restaurant and Oyster Bar

¼ cup Meyer lemon juice	½ cup shaved Vella Mezzo
½ cup extra virgin olive oil	Secco Jack
Salt and pepper	1 bunch chives
6 baby artichokes, raw	

In a small bowl, add the lemon juice and whisk in the olive oil until a creamy infusion is achieved. Add salt and pepper to taste. Peel off the outer green leaves of the artichokes until the yellow leaves are exposed. Trim the tip and stem until yellow flesh is exposed. Thinly slice the artichokes and toss in the lemon dressing with Jack. Top with chopped chives.

4 servings

Fiesta and Pacific Markets

Family-owned Fiesta and Pacific Market are two of Sonoma County's favorite grocery stores. In 1945, the late Stanley and Mary Mohar established the family's first market, the original Pacific Market at the corner of Kentucky and Washington Streets in Petaluma. A son, Stanley Jr., or Moe, became a partner as the Mohar's empire grew to five grocery stores including a well-loved Food City Market in the Roseland area of Santa Rosa.

Moe left Food City to open Sebastopol's Fiesta Market, in 1966. He put his two sons and three nephews to work in the bustling new market. Eventually, three grandsons, Brad Mohar and his cousins Gary and Ken Silveira, became the proud owners of Fiesta Market in 1986 and Moe retired. The trio opened a new Santa Rosa store with an old name, Pacific Market, in 1998. Brad's brother Rick rejoined the Pacific Market team after selling his own retail wine business.

Today Fiesta and Pacific showcase the excellent products grown, raised and produced in Sonoma County. The stores were among the first in the United States to add a dedicated organic produce section. Full service meat and fresh fish departments feature specialties like free-range chicken, local farmed oysters, line caught salmon, house made sausages and marinated, tumbled meat.

Fiesta fires up the only authentic crab pot in use north of San Francisco. The wine department, run by Brad's wife Kristi, stocks a huge international and local selection. The cheese department, a full service deli, an authentic sushi bar, a giant salad, soup and olive bar, hot rotisserie chicken counter and a fully stocked bakery are also available.

The dedication to excellent service and products has earned the larger Fiesta Market recognition as Sebastopol's Business of the Year as well as being named The Best Market in Sonoma County in a newspaper reader's poll every year since 1994. Smaller Pacific Market has taken the 2nd place spot in that poll since its opening.

Fiesta Market: 550 Gravenstein Hwy, (Hwy. 116)
west of downtown Sebastopol 707.823.4916
Pacific Market: Pacific & Bryden Lanes,
in the Town & Country Center, Santa Rosa 707.546.FOOD
fiestamkt.com or pacificmkt.com.

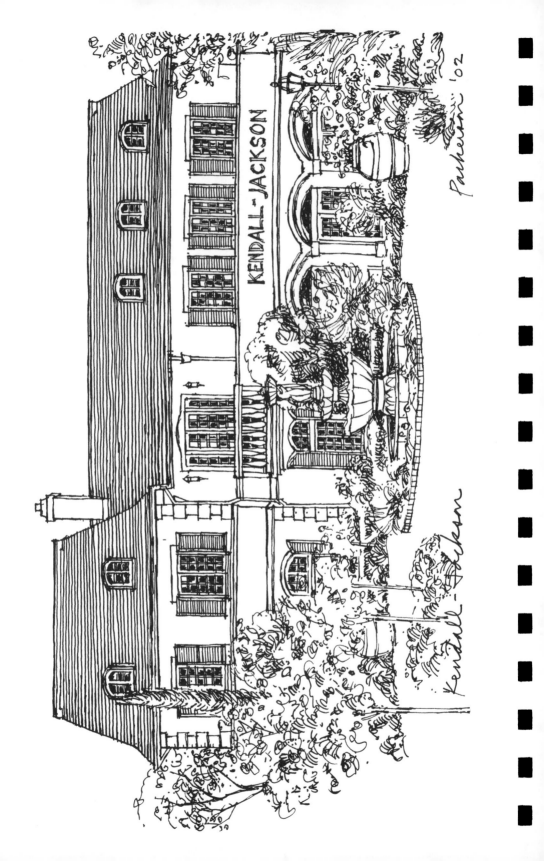

Kendall Jackson
Wine Estates

Kendall-Jackson Wine Estates is a family-owned farming and winemaking company based in Sonoma County. One of the great pleasures of living here is the chance to match our wines with the bounty of local food products.

In a short 20 years, Kendall-Jackson has grown from Jess Jackson's back yard project to become America's favorite varietal wine. While K-J is best known for its Chardonnay, which became America's favorite soon after its debut in 1983, the company now makes a wide range of wine throughout California and around the world.

Kendall Jackson wines consistently win critical praise because farming is our foundation. We seek out the best North Coast vineyards to grow our grapes. They ferment and age in small oak barrels, while winemakers taste and compare each lot before selecting the final blend.

We never lose sight of how our wines match with the natural products of Sonoma County. At the Kendall-Jackson Wine Center near Fulton, the Organic Culinary Gardens acquaint visitors with the flavor affinities between wine and food.

Consumers have come to expect delightful flavors in the Kendall-Jackson Wine Estates portfolio of premium wines. The Kendall-Jackson brand itself features Vintners Reserve®, Grand Reserve, Great Estates™ and Stature™ wines. KJWE also offers the Camelot and Pepi brands with California appellations, Sonoma County's La Crema Winery, Edmeades from Mendocino County, Yangarra Park from Australia, Calina from Chile and Tapiz from Argentina.

Get more information on the web at www.kj.com or better yet. . . visit the Kendall-Jackson Wine Center Tasting Room and Culinary Garden at:
5007 Fulton Road
Fulton, California 95439
Phone: 707-571-8100

POULTRY

DUCK CONFIT
WITH LENTIL RATATOUILLE

Chef Laurie Souza, Korbel Champagne Cellars

1 tablespoon juniper berries
2 tablespoons black
　peppercorns
2 star anise
2 cloves
¼ cup coarse salt
1 teaspoon ground coriander
¼ teaspoon ground nutmeg

1 tablespoon minced garlic
2 bay leaves, crumbled
3 tablespoons chopped fresh
　thyme
2 tablespoons chopped fresh
　parsley
8 duck legs
Rendered duck fat

This dish must be prepared with rendered duck fat. Try buying it at specialty food stores, butchers or duck farms. It can be strained and used again and again. If you would like to render your own, remove as much skin and fat as possible from the duck, process it in a food processor and place in a heavy pot and melt the fat. Skim the top and refrigerate until ready to use.

Grind the first 5 spices in a spice grinder. Mix with the rest of the ingredients to make a marinade. Rub the marinade over the duck pieces, cover and refrigerate for 24 hours. Then wipe off most of the marinade and place the duck in a deep baking pan. Cover all of the duck pieces with rendered fat. Put in a cold oven and turn oven on to 275 degrees. Cook for about 4 hours. The meat will start to pull away from the end of the leg when done. When the duck is cool enough to handle, remove it from the fat. Strain fat and reserve for next use. The duck may be taken off the bone and shredded or left whole. To serve whole, roast or grill the duck until the skin is crisp. The meat will keep in the refrigerator for up to 6 days or you can freeze it.

LENTIL RATATOUILLE

2 cups dried French lentils
½ onion, finely diced
3 cups chicken stock or water
3 garlic cloves, minced
4 carrots, peeled and finely
　diced

4 zucchini (green part only),
　finely diced
1 sweet red pepper, finely
　diced
1 yellow pepper, finely diced
Dried thyme, salt and black
　pepper to taste

Place lentils, onion and liquid in a saucepan. Bring to a boil and then simmer for 20 to 25 minutes. Sauté each of the remaining vegetables separately in olive oil, a pinch of thyme, a pinch of minced garlic, salt and black pepper until soft. When lentils are done, drain and add to the sautéed vegetables.

8 servings

GENERAL TAO'S CHICKEN

Chef Gary Chu, Gary Chu's Gourmet Chinese Cuisine

FOR CHICKEN

1 pound leg of chicken meat
   sliced in 2-inch long and
   ½-inch wide strips
1 egg

1¼ teaspoons ginger powder
1¼ teaspoons garlic powder
7½ teaspoons cornstarch

Place chicken in a bowl. Add all other ingredients and mix well. Deep fry. Set aside.

FOR SAUCE

5 teaspoons smoke-flavored
   barbecue sauce
5 teaspoons A-1 Sauce
2½ teaspoons soy sauce
2½ teaspoons vinegar

2 tablespoons sugar
2½ teaspoons honey
2½ teaspoons dry sherry
7½ teaspoons chicken broth

Mix ingredients and set aside.

PREPARATION

2 tablespoons canola oil
4-5 small dry chili pods
1 tablespoon fresh ground
   ginger

1 tablespoon fresh minced garlic
1 tablespoon chili paste
1 tablespoon fresh chopped
   green onions

Heat wok with canola oil and add next 5 ingredients. Add sauce and fried chicken. Stir well and top with a few drops of sesame and chili oils.

ROCKY THE RANGE CHICKEN COCOTTE GRANDE-MERE

Chef Elizabeth A. Ozanich, Brasserie de la Mer

4 skin-on boneless Rocky the
  Range Chicken breasts
Salt and pepper
8 ounces reduced chicken
  stock
1 pound fingerling potatoes

2 ounces applewood smoked
  bacon lardons
1 pound braised greens
4 ounces forest mushrooms
3 ounces caramelized onions
4 ounces sauce marchand du vin

FOR SAUCE MARCHAND DU VIN

1 bottle red wine
4 whole shallots
3 cups veal stock

2 ounces fresh thyme
1 bay leaf
Salt and pepper

Season chicken breasts with salt and pepper. Brown the breast skin side down in sauté pan. Turn over breasts and place in a small earthenware ovenproof dish. Place in a preheated 400 degree oven and roast until 120 degrees internal temperature. Add chicken stock, potatoes, bacon lardons, greens, mushrooms and caramelized onions and finish cooking the chicken. The internal temperature should be 165 degrees.

FOR SAUCE MARCHAND

Chop shallots and put them and the bottle of red wine in a nonreactive sauce pan. Add thyme and bay leaf. Set burner on high and reduce wine by half. In a separate pan reduce veal stock by half. Combine the two reductions and strain through a fine mesh strainer. Reduce to a nice sauce consistency and season with salt and pepper.

TO SERVE

Divide up the chicken and vegetables and serve in a shallow pasta plates. Ladle sauce marchand du vin over each breast and serve.

4 servings

CHICKEN BREAST GRAZIANO

Chef Graziano Perozzi, Graziano's Ristorante

4 skinless and boneless
    chicken breasts
Flour
4 slices Monterey Jack cheese
8 slices Italian prosciutto

1 avocado
4 tablespoons olive oil
1 tablespoon chopped shallots
Pinch of white pepper
6 ounces white wine

Butterfly chicken in two, pound flat and flour. Set aside. Layer one slice of cheese, add prosciutto and two slices of avocado for each piece of chicken. Set aside. Heat oil, add chicken and let sauté 2 minutes on each side. Pour off oil and add shallots, white pepper and white wine. Cook on high for 30 seconds to a minute. Remove from heat. Layer chicken with cheese, prosciutto and avocado. Put in a preheated oven at 400 degrees for 1 minute, until cheese is melted.

4 servings

CHICKEN CACCIATORE

Chef Angelo Ibleto, Angelo's Italian Taste

1 pound chicken
2-3 garlic cloves
Olive oil
1 onion, chopped
1 bell pepper, chopped

1 cup fresh sliced mushrooms
1 14.5-ounce can Italian
    tomatoes
1 jar Angelo's Italian Salsa

Brown chicken and garlic cloves in olive oil. Add onion, bell pepper, mushrooms, tomatoes and Angelo's Italian Salsa. Simmer until done, approximately 1 hour. Serve over rice.

8 servings

DUCK WITH PLUM SAUCE

Chef Jessica Gorin, **J** Wine Company

2 medium white onions
3 carrots, peeled
1 large leek, white and tender
  green only
2 tablespoons olive oil
2 cups red wine, **J** Pinot Noir
  or Pinotage
4 cups chicken stock
  (preferably roasted chicken
  stock)

12 Santa Rosa plums, seeded
  and chopped
2 tablespoons sugar
1 teaspoon red wine vinegar
4 Sonoma duck breasts,
  cleaned and trimmed
Salt and pepper

For sauce: Coarsely chop the onion, carrot and leek and sweat in a pot with olive oil and a pinch of salt. When the vegetables begin to get color on their edges, add the red wine and reduce by half. Add the stock and simmer for 1 hour, skimming the top as needed. While the sauce reduces, in another pot, cook the plums with the sugar until softened, being careful not to let the sugar burn. Add vinegar and cook for another 5 minutes. After the stock has simmered for an hour, pour it through a colander into the pot with the plums. Continue to reduce the sauce until it has a nice, thick consistency. Strain out plums.

For duck: Preheat oven to 400 degrees. Liberally season both sides of each duck breast with salt and pepper. Put one oven-safe large pan over high heat. When pan is hot, add the duck, skin side down. Immediately lower flame to low-medium. Render the fat out of the skin until the skin becomes golden. Move duck to oven for about 3 minutes. Flip duck and continue to cook for 3 to 5 minutes. Let duck rest before slicing.

Serve with roasted potatoes and sautéed chard for a rich summer dinner.

4 servings

THREE-CHEESE CHICKEN BREASTS IN TOMATO SAUCE

Vella Cheese Company

¼ cup olive oil
6 skinless boneless chicken
   breast halves
Salt and pepper
½ large onion, chopped
2 large garlic cloves, chopped
1 tablespoon dried oregano
1 15-ounce can tomato sauce
1 14½-ounce can Italian-style
   stewed tomatoes

⅓ cup dry white wine
2 bay leaves
8 ounces penne, freshly
   cooked
1 cup grated Vella Part Skim
   Jack
⅓ cup grated Vella Asiago
⅓ cup grated Vella Dry
   Monterey Jack

Preheat oven to 375 degrees. Butter 13 x 8 x 2-inch glass baking dish. Heat oil in heavy large skillet over high heat. Season chicken with salt and pepper. Add chicken to skillet. Sauté until outside is white, about 1 minute per side. Transfer to plate. Add onion, garlic and oregano to skillet and sauté until onion begins to soften, about 4 minutes. Add tomato sauce, stewed tomatoes with their juices, wine and bay leaves and cook until sauce thickens, breaking up tomatoes with spoon, about 8 minutes. Discard bay leaves. Line prepared dish with penne. Arrange chicken over. Spoon sauce over, covering chicken and pasta completely. Mix cheeses in small bowl. Sprinkle cheeses over sauce. Bake until chicken is just cooked through and sauce bubbles, about 20 minutes.

6 servings

STUFFED BREAST OF CHICKEN

Chef Lisa Hemenway, Lisa Hemenway's Bistro

4 breasts chicken, skinless	½ cup Asiago cheese
8 green chard leaves	2 tablespoons chopped fresh
1 small yellow onion, minced	basil
1 small leek, minced	Salt and pepper to taste
3 tablespoons olive oil	1 pinch nutmeg
1 cup ricotta	1 cup white wine

Place chicken breasts between plastic wrap and pound to ¼-inch thickness. Set aside. Bring 2 quarts salted water to a boil. Blanch chard leaves bout 3 minutes. Pull from hot water and run under cold water. Set aside. Sauté onion with leek for 3 minutes in olive oil. Remove from heat. In a small bowl place ricotta, Asiago, basil, salt, pepper and nutmeg. Blend with spatula. Add sautéed onion and leeks. Take 4 chard leaves and finely chop. Add to mix.

To assemble: Lay one full chard leaf over each chicken breast. Place ¼ of ricotta mixture on top of each leaf. Roll each breast tightly and lay in a baking pan, seam side down. Sprinkle white wine over breasts. Add salt and pepper, and bake at 375 degrees for 20 minutes. Check at the 10 minute point and baste the top of the breasts. When finished cooking, remove from oven and let rest for 3 minutes. Slice with sharp knife and fan.

4 servings

WINDSOR'S RASPBERRY GAME HENS

Windsor Vineyards

2 cups raspberries
¼ cup Windsor Zinfandel
2 tablespoons olive oil
1 teaspoon Dijon mustard

1 teaspoon sugar
1 teaspoon thyme
Salt and pepper to taste
4 Rock Cornish game hens

Purée the raspberries in a blender or food processor, and strain through a sieve to remove the seeds. Whisk in wine, oil, mustard, sugar, thyme, salt and pepper. Pour the mixture over game hens and marinate overnight.

Preheat oven to 400 degrees. Drain the marinade into a bowl, then place birds skin side up in a roasting pan and roast for about 40 minutes. Brush birds with reserved marinade at least twice during roasting.

4 servings

TEA SMOKED DUCK

Chef Gary Chu, Gary Chu's Gourmet Chinese Cuisine

Enough uncooked rice to
    cover bottom of a wok
1 stalk fresh sugar cane
Equal amounts of dried oolong
    tea
Equal amounts of orange slices
Enough fresh bamboo shoots
    to cover top of steamer

1 4-5 pound fresh duck
3 anise stars
1 teaspoon Szechwan
    peppercorns
1 stalk green onion, julienne
2 slices fresh ginger
2 tablespoons salt

Cover bottom of wok in layers of rice, sugar cane, tea and orange slices. Place a large steamer in wok and layer steamer with bamboo shoots. Place duck on top of bamboo shoots and turn up heat until the ingredients start to smoke and duck skin turns brown. Remove wok from heat. Remove duck and stuff cavity with anise, peppercorns, green onion, ginger and salt. Steam duck for 1 hour and 15 minutes.

Eat hot or refrigerate. To reheat, place duck in 350 degree oven for 15 minutes.

ERNIE'S CHICKEN

Jan Rosen, Executive Chef, J.M. Rosen's Waterfront Grill

This recipe was developed by Jan Rosen as a tribute for Frank Sinatra's long time personal assistant's husband. Mr. Sinatra gave the Tomato Sauce Recipe to Jan Rosen to be used in this dish.

1 medium eggplant
Salt
2 eggs beaten
1 cup breadcrumbs
   (Italian seasoned)
4 boneless chicken breasts

Clarified butter
Flour
Mozzarella cheese
Frank Sinatra's Tomato Sauce
   (recipe follows)

Peel eggplant and slice into 1-inch rounds. Salt and set aside to remove excess moisture. After several hours, rinse well, pat dry and dip eggplant into the two beaten eggs. Heavily dust with Italian seasoned breadcrumbs. Sauté until golden.

Lightly dust the chicken breasts with flour. Sauté in clarified butter until each side is seared. Place sautéed eggplant round on top of each breast. Top with Frank Sinatra's Tomato Sauce and mozzarella cheese. Place in oven for 10 minutes at 400 degrees. Serve to oohs and aahs!

4 servings

FRANK SINATRA'S TOMATO SAUCE RECIPE

Jan Rosen, Executive Chef, J.M. Rosen's Waterfront Grill

2 tablespoons olive oil
¼ onion, cut crescent shaped
4 cloves garlic

1 #2½ can Italian peeled
   tomatoes
Fresh basil and oregano
Salt and pepper

Heat the olive oil in a pan. Add onion and garlic. Sauté until brown and remove the garlic. Put the tomatoes in a blender with a small amount of liquid from the can and mix gently for less than a minute. Slowly add the tomatoes to the mixture in the pan, being very careful pouring the liquid on the oil. Add fresh basil and oregano, salt and pepper and simmer for 15 minutes.

FOIE GRAS POACHED IN WALNUT BROTH WITH BABY DRIED MORELS

Laurent Manrique, Sonoma Saveur

½ cup baby dried morels
½ cup Vin de Voile from
    Gaillac or Vin Jaune from
    Jura
4 ounces walnut oil, divided
1¾ pounds foie gras
Cold milk

1 quart duck bouillon
8 cloves garlic confit in duck
    fat
30-35 pieces fresh walnuts
Sea salt
Fresh black pepper

Clean the morels making sure extra sand is out. Soak them for 4 hours in the white wine and ½ of the walnut oil.

Soak the whole foie gras in cold milk for 2 hours to extract the blood. Remove the foie gras from the milk and pat dry. Season the foie gras well and let the salt penetrate into it. Let sit at room temperature.

In a large pot, simmer the duck bouillon with garlic cloves, walnuts, morels and wine from the morels for about 15 minutes. Place the foie gras into the pot making sure the broth covers the foie gras. Simmer (do not boil) for 20 to 30 minutes. Make sure the livers are medium. At this point, delicately take the foie gras out of the pot and place on a linen cloth. Strain the bouillon.

Arrange the morels, garlic confit and walnuts in a soup bowl. Slice the foie gras. Sprinkle sea salt and plenty of black pepper on the foie gras. Blend the broth and walnut oil until it is emulsified. Serve very hot on top of the foie gras.

8 servings

FOIE GRAS ROASTED IN FIG LEAVES

with Fig-Port Sauce and Green Almonds (Land/Forrest)

Laurent Manrique, Sonoma Saveur

2 cups whole dried figs	2 cups veal or chicken stock
4 cups ruby port	1 lobe foie gras (about 8 ounces)
1 cup milk	1 large fig leaf
¼ cup green almonds	Salt and pepper

Combine the figs and port in a large bowl. Cover and refrigerate overnight. Combine milk and green almonds in a small bowl. Stir in a pinch of salt. Cover and refrigerate overnight.

The next day, strain the port, reserving both the figs and the liquid. Quarter the figs and set aside. Pour the port into a heavy small saucepan. Bring to a boil and reduce by ¾. Add the stock and reduce by half Add the figs, season with salt and pepper, and set aside. Drain the almonds and discard the milk.

Preheat oven to 400 degrees. Heat a heavy small skillet over high heat. Season the foie gras with salt and pepper. Add to the skillet and sear on all sides, shaking the pan to keep from sticking, about 4 to 5 minutes. Place the foie gras in the center of the fig leaf, add the fat from the skillet to the port sauce. Wrap the fig leaf around the foie gras, enclosing completely. Tie with kitchen string into a tight bundle. Place the foie gras on a baking sheet. Roast in the oven until a skewer inserted into the thickest part feels warm when removed, about 10 minutes. Transfer the wrapped foie gras to a cutting board and let stand 5 minutes.

To serve: Unwrap the foie gras and cut into 8 slices. Place 2 slices on each of 4 plates. Spoon the sauce and the figs over. Sprinkle with green almonds and serve.

4 servings

Sonoma Saveurs

A new and unique culinary experience called Sonoma Saveurs opened its doors on the historic Sonoma Plaza in the spring of 2003, further adding to the food and wine culture of this charming wine country town. This is a new venture with the owners of Sonoma Foie Gras, Junny and Guillermo Gonzalez, who have been the only western United States foie gras producers for the past 17 years, and a team of French chefs and entrepreneurs.

One of these partners is Chef Laurent Manrique, a celebrity chef previously in New York and now in San Francisco. He was born and raised in the foie gras region of southwest France, and is a passionate ambassador of this culinary specialty.

Sonoma Saveurs has created a new line of specialty foods with a decidedly Mediterranean influence, from the newly released "Artisan Foie Gras," produced using the traditional methods of centuries past, to duck meat products, a selection of local tastes from wine country producers, and a future line of bistro dishes.

Sonoma Saveurs showcases its food in a tasting delicatessen/rotisserie with "a la provencale" décor, where guests sample a selection of products, paired with coordinating wines, in either the indoor tasting rooms or on an outdoor patio. Products are also offered for sale in the boutique section to take home, or from the website or catalogue.

The goal of Sonoma Saveur is to offer guests an exciting and pleasurable culinary experience through the tasting and exposure to novel "saveurs" in a unique historical setting. Your visit will be welcome.

487 First Street West
Sonoma, CA 95476
707-538-2915

www.sonomasaveurs.com

Cucina Paradiso Ristorante Italiano

Tucked away near the Petaluma River turning basin is an intimate hideaway with a four star chef. Cucina Paradiso combines the freshest and most seasonal herbs, spices, fruits and vegetables into hot and cold surprises for the palate's enjoyment.

Lamb and chicken recipes reflect the most tender products available from local hillsides and fish, fresh from just a few miles away, is chosen daily by the chef. Only the finest cut and quality of beef is served at Cucina Paradiso.

Sauces accompany most entrees and may be delicate or spirituous, your choice. The wine list boasts an exceptional selection of local and Italian offerings.

Family owned and operated by chef Dennis and Maria, customer service is their pleasure. Reservations are recommended.

Cucino Paradiso
56 East Washington Street
Petaluma, CA 94952
(707) 782-1139

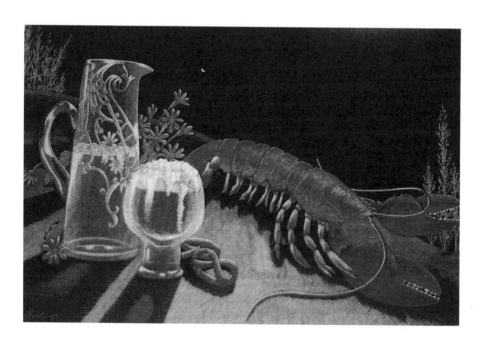

Petaluma Market

Petaluma Market, a favorite for Petaluma shoppers, is known for its quality and its extensive selection. Fresh produce from local farms, including a substantial organic selection, is offered. Top quality meats and seafood and wholesome daily products plus the traditional large grocery selection are featured.

Petaluma Market is also known for its full deli and a gourmet selection of sought-after wines as well as a comprehensive offering of cheeses, all essential to your party planning.

Petaluma Market is also committed to the local community, particularly support of schools. Visit our website for information.

210 Western Avenue, Petaluma, CA
(707) 762-8452

www.petalumamarket.com

Petaluma Poultry

A pioneer in Sonoma County agriculture, raising natural and organic poultry, Petaluma Poultry is currently led by President Darrel Freitas and CFO Dave Martinelli. The company was founded in 1989 by Allen Shainsky.

In the 1980's Petaluma Poultry created an all-vegetarian diet based on corn and soy, free of antibiotics and animal byproducts. Rocky the Range Chicken and Rocky Jr., are raised on this diet in spacious ranch houses. Rocky the Range Chicken exercises outdoors, and Rosie is the first certified organic chicken in the country.

Petaluma Poultry uses sustainable practices in all phases of business, and this year received the Environmental Business of the Year Award from the Sonoma County Conservation Council.

1-800-556-6789
petalumapoultry.com

Sebastopol

Laguna

MEATS

VITELLO CON FUNGHI

Veal with Oyster Mushrooms

Chef Michael Ghilarducci, The Depot Hotel, Cucina Rustica

12 1½-ounce slices veal, pounded until flat
4 tablespoons oil
Salt and pepper
Flour
1 pound sliced white oyster mushrooms (cultivated oyster or Shiitake mushrooms may be substituted, if necessary)

3 tablespoons shallots, diced
½ cup dry sherry
1½ cups heavy cream
½ cup veal demi-glace sauce (optional)

Heat the oil in a large skillet. Salt and pepper the veal to taste and dredge lightly in flour, shaking off the excess. Sauté each scaloppini of veal until slightly brown on each side, 30 seconds to a minute. Do not overcook. Remove veal from pan and add the mushrooms to the same pan. Sauté until tender. Add the shallots, sauté 1 minute, and deglaze the pan with the sherry. Add the cream and the demi-glace, if it is to be used. Cook until slightly thickened. Adjust seasoning, return the veal and its juices to the pan, warm slightly and then arrange the veal on the plate and pour the sauce over to serve.

4 servings

EASTSIDE'S FAMOUS BARBECUED RIBS

Chef Randy Summerville, Rosen's EastSide Grill

Great for holiday parties

10 pounds ribs

Randy's Famous Barbecue Sauce (recipe follows)

BRINE
Liquid (may be citrus juice)
Salt

Sugar to taste

Use 1 part salt to 9 parts liquid. Add sugar as desired. Soak ribs in brine for 8 hours. Place ribs on charcoal grill for 45 minutes. Then bake for 12 hours in 150 degree oven. Take ribs out and lightly coat with barbecue sauce. Cover with foil and place back in oven at 150 degrees until ready to serve.

RANDY'S FAMOUS BARBECUE SAUCE

Chef Randy Summerville, Rosen's EastSide Grill

4 Anaheim chilies	¼ pound brown sugar
4 pasilla chilies	1 cup apricot preserves
2½ yellow onions	½ cup molasses
Olive oil	½ tablespoon chipotle chilies
6½ cups canned chili sauce	⅛ cup Worcestershire sauce
6½ cups ketchup	⅛ cup Dijon mustard

Sauté Anaheim chilies, pasillas and onions in olive oil. Add remaining ingredients and cook for 15 minutes. Cool and then purée.

5 quarts

BISTTECCA DI MANZO CON BURRO DE GORGONZOLA

New York Steak with Gorgonzola Butter

Chef Maria Belmonte, Caffé Portofino

6 tablespoons butter, divided	½ lemon
¼ cup crumbled mild Gorgonzola cheese	4 12-ounce tender steaks
	1 tablespoon salt
1 tablespoon chopped parsley	Pepper to taste

Put 4 tablespoons of butter, Gorgonzola, parsley, and a few drops of lemon juice into a bowl and beat with a wooden spoon until mixture is smooth and creamy. Roll mixture into a cylinder, wrap in foil, and cover for 1 hour. Melt remaining 2 tablespoons of butter in a pan, add the steaks and cook over high heat for 2 minutes on each side. Drain, season with salt and pepper and put on a serving dish. Cut Gorgonzola butter into 12 slices and put 3 slices on each steak. Serve at once.

4 servings

PORK TENDERLOIN WITH RASPBERRY SAUCE

Chef Phil McGauley, Korbel Champagne Cellars

MARINADE

¼ cup olive oil	½ teaspoon salt
1 teaspoon thyme	Freshly ground pepper
½ teaspoon sage	

PORK

2 pounds pork tenderloin	2 teaspoons raspberry vinegar
Flour for dusting	3 tablespoons raspberry purée
2 tablespoons clarified butter	1 tablespoon soy sauce
1 cup sliced mushrooms	3 tablespoons brandy
1 teaspoon minced shallots	Salt and pepper to taste
1½ cups veal stock	

Trim pork of any fat and silverskin. Marinate pork overnight. Remove from marinade, pat dry, lightly dust with flour and sauté in butter until brown on all sides. DO NOT OVERCOOK. Remove pork and set aside. Remove any excess oil from pan. Add a little more butter, mushrooms and shallots, sauté until soft, not brown. Add stock, vinegar, raspberry purée, soy sauce, brandy and reduce until desired consistency. Place sauce onto plate. Slice pork on a bias, arrange about five cuts standing up on top of sauce. Garnish with fresh raspberry and orange zest.

GARLIC AND HERB ROASTED TENDERLOIN OF BEEF

Chef Jeff Young, Alexander Valley Vineyards

1 beef head filet
6 cloves peeled garlic
1 tablespoon each rosemary,
    oregano and thyme

¼ cup olive oil
Salt and pepper

Have your butcher trim out a 2½ to 3 pound beef filet roast including the silver skin, then have him truss it up. Place garlic, herbs, salt and pepper in a food processor and run, adding olive oil in a thin stream until finely minced. Rub beef thoroughly with garlic and herb mixture and refrigerate overnight. Remove beef from refrigerator and let sit at room temperature for half an hour before searing in a hot pan. Place in preheated oven at 400 degrees and cook for 20 minutes or until thermometer reads 140 degrees. Remove and let rest for 10 minutes. Slice and serve with your favorite accompaniments.

4 to 6 servings

Near Fort Ross

SOUVLAKI

Chef Christine Topolos, Russian River Vineyards

Souvlaki is Greek marinated lamb on a skewer (en brochette sounds classier). Perhaps you know it as shish kabob or shashlik. The essence of a great souvlaki is a great marinade.

1½ pounds lamb leg, cut in well-trimmed cubes	½ cup lemon juice
¼ cup minced garlic (!!!)	1 tablespoon coarse ground black pepper
½ cup Greek olive oil	1 tablespoon Greek oregano

Combine the last 5 ingredients and marinate the lamb in this mixture for 3 days in a shallow glass or porcelain bowl, turning once a day. Skewer and just before cooking sprinkle lightly with salt or with Greek seasoning.

Skewer the lamb and grill or broil turning to brown evenly. Vegetables may be added between the cubes of meat, but at Russian River Vineyards we follow the most common Greek practice and use meat only. If you would like to, skewer vegetables and grill them on the side. Vegetables and meat don't require the same cooking time. The length of time needed to cook the lamb will depend entirely on your broiler or grill, but will not exceed 2 minutes a side. Think of the skewer as having 4 sides, 5 to 8 minutes all together. Aim for medium rare. The marinade has already tenderized and partially cooked the meat. An over-cooked souvlaki will be hard to the touch and dry and tough in the mouth.

This is an all purpose marinade and is very good on pork or chicken as well as lamb.

Notes on the ingredients: Yes, that is a lot of garlic; cut it back if you must. Thankfully, good quality minced garlic is now available in jars. Make sure you are buying fresh minced garlic, and not rehydrated dried garlic. I prefer the garlic packed in oil to that packed in water. Greek olive oil is not essential, any good virgin olive oil will suffice, but Greek oregano is. Look for it in natural food, gourmet, or specialty food stores. Generic (Italian) oregano can be used, but the result will not be the same.

4 servings

LAMB MOUSSAKA

Chef Robin Lehnhoff, Lake Sonoma Winery

3 pounds fresh ground lamb
4 tablespoons olive oil
1 tablespoon chopped fresh
  garlic
1 large zucchini squash, diced
1 large crookneck squash,
  diced
1 large onion, chopped
1 large eggplant, diced
1 teaspoon ground cinnamon
½ teaspoon ground cloves
½ teaspoon ground mace
1 teaspoon crushed chili flakes
1-2 teaspoons kosher salt
1 teaspoon black pepper
½ cup all purpose flour
  (amount may vary)
8 ounces sheep's milk feta
  cheese
4 cups breadcrumbs
1 teaspoon dried oregano
1 teaspoon dried thyme

Sauté lamb in olive oil until completely cooked. Drain off excess fat. Add to lamb, the squash, onion, garlic and eggplant. Cook until vegetables are translucent and add spices, salt and pepper. Sprinkle flour over lamb mixture to absorb oil and fat. This will bind the moussaka together. Pour into casserole dish and set aside.

Combine feta, breadcrumbs and herbs in mixer fitted with a paddle. Mix ingredients until you form a crumbly mixture. Lightly drizzle this over the lamb making sure to cover the meat completely. Cover casserole with foil and bake for 1 hour at 350 degrees. Remove foil and lightly brown the top before serving.

6 to 8 servings

BROWN SUGAR-CHILI RUBBED BABY BACK RIBS

Chef Jeff Young, Alexander Valley Vineyards

⅓ cup brown sugar
2 tablespoons chili powder

1 tablespoon kosher salt
1 rack pork baby back ribs

Place first 3 ingredients in a food processor and mix well. Place ribs on a sheet pan and cover with spice mixture. Cover and refrigerate overnight. Grill over indirect heat for 1½ to 2 hours or until tender.

2 servings (in the chef's case, 1)

SLOW-ROASTED PORK

with Garlic, Fennel and Wild Fennel Pollen

Michele Anna Jordan

3½ pounds boneless pork
  shoulder or butt, preferably
  Niman Ranch
3 tablespoons kosher salt, plus
  more to taste
6 garlic bulbs, outer skins
  removed

6 medium fennel bulbs, trimmed
1 tablespoon wild fennel
  pollen, available in local
  markets such as Oakville
  Grocery
Black pepper in a mill
Lemon wedges for garnish

If you have a clay roaster, soak it according to the manufacturer's instructions.

Rub the salt into the pork, using all of the salt. Place the pork in the clay roaster or roasting pan, add 1 cup water and put in a cold oven. Set the heat to 300 degrees and cook for 2 hours. Remove from the oven, add the garlic bulbs and fennel bulbs, season the vegetables and meat with the fennel pollen, return to the oven and bake for 1½ hours, or until the fennel and garlic are completely tender and the pork falls apart when pressed.

Drain off the fat that has collected in the roaster or pan, cover and let rest 10 minutes. Use two forks to pull the pork apart into big chunks. Set on a platter, surround with the garlic and fennel, season with salt and pepper, garnish with lemon wedges and serve immediately.

4 to 6 servings

GRILLED LEG OF LAMB

Marinated in Vanilla and Rosemary

Chef Ralph Tingle, Bistro Ralph

A mint au jus goes nicely with this recipe, but is not necessary. Roasted creamer potatoes and roasted garlic cloves mixed with herbs makes a nice rustic complimentary starch.

1 leg of spring lamb, butterflied
½ cup whole fresh rosemary leaves
3 tablespoons chopped mint leaves

6 cloves garlic, finely chopped
6 tablespoons vanilla extract
1 pint vanilla yogurt (with active cultures)

Mix all marinade ingredients in a bowl and evenly coat leg of lamb on both sides. Place in a baking dish to marinate 24 to 48 hours refrigerated. The active culture yogurt will help to tenderize the meat. Before grilling, remove most of the marinade and let lamb rest out of refrigerator to raise to room temperature. Grill over moderately hot coals until medium rare, about 12 minutes per side. Let rest about 10 minutes before slicing thinly and serving.

8 to 10 servings

ROBERT'S OSSO BUCO

Chef Robert Steiner, DeSchmire Restaurant

This is one of my favorite winter night dishes, but excellent any time of year.

6 2-inch thick veal osso buco
   cuts
Salt and pepper
5 tablespoons olive oil
1 large yellow onion, finely
   chopped
2 carrots, finely chopped
6 garlic cloves, chopped
6 ounces tomato paste
1 tablespoon flour

2 cups red wine
2 quarts plump ripe canned
   tomatoes
2 ounces orange juice
   concentrate
½ bunch parsley
1 orange, zest
1 lemon, zest
¼ cube butter

Season meat with salt and pepper. Place heavy braising pan on top of stove. Add olive oil and place osso buco meat in pan and brown on both sides. Add chopped onion, carrots and garlic and sauté for 3 minutes. Add tomato paste, flour, wine, tomatoes and orange juice concentrate. Mix thoroughly and let simmer for 15 minutes. Place this in oven and braise at 330 degrees for 1½ to 2 hours or until meat pulls away from the bone. Make a gremolata from orange and lemon zest and the chopped parsley. Place ingredients into sauté pan with butter and sauté for 1 minute. Remove meat from oven and degrease any excess fat. Place osso buco on platter and sprinkle gremolata over top. Serve with risotto or mashed potatoes and greens.

6 servings

De Schmir Restaurant - Petaluma

Parkinson '95

Parkinson '95

SANGIOVESE BRAISED VEAL SHANK

Chef Jeff Young, Alexander Valley Vineyards

6 pieces veal shank
Olive oil
Salt and pepper
2 carrots, peeled and diced

1 onion, diced
2 turnips, peeled and diced
1 parsnip, peeled and diced
1 cup AVV Estate Sangiovese

Preheat a large sauté pan to medium high. Salt and pepper veal, add enough oil to coat bottom of pan. Arrange the veal shanks in the sauté pan and brown. Remove to a roasting pan large enough so there is one layer. Add vegetables to sauté pan and cook for 5 minutes. Next add wine to vegetables and deglaze pan. Pour this over the veal and add enough water to just cover. Cook in a 375 degree oven for 2 to 2½ hours or until meat is gently falling off bone. Remove meat to a warm platter, strain vegetables and stock into a saucepot. Reduce liquid until slightly thickened. Serve with Gorgonzola polenta or saffron rice.

6 servings

GRILLED SONOMA LAMB CHOPS

with Aubergine and Soy Glaze

Chef Gary Arthur, Terrace Grill at Flamingo Resort Hotel

12 lamb chops
8 ounces fresh carrot juice
2 ounces fresh ginger

1 tablespoon ground turmeric
2 tablespoons sesame oil

Mix all ingredients together and marinate for 2 hours minimum.

SOY GLAZE

3 tablespoons light soy sauce
  (tamari)
1 tablespoon Chinese rice
  wine
1 tablespoon sesame oil

2 tablespoons rice vinegar
1 green onion, chopped
2 cloves garlic, chopped
1 teaspoon chili bean paste
  (toban jiang)

Mix all ingredients together and keep overnight.

Slice and steam 3 long Asian eggplants. Grill the chops and arrange on top of eggplant once it is fully cooked. Discard all water. Pour the soy glaze over the top and serve immediately.

4 servings

PORK TENDERLOIN MEDALLIONS

Stuffed with Wild Mushrooms Served with Pomegranate Sauce

Chef Carlo Cavallo, Meritage Restaurant and Oyster Bar

1 cup wild mushrooms, chopped and sautéed with white wine
3 tablespoons minced parsley
⅓ cup breadcrumbs
¼ cup grated Parmesan cheese
¼ cup shredded fontina cheese
1 egg
2 pork tenderloins (3 pounds), cleaned

Salt and pepper
3 tablespoons chopped sage
3 tablespoons chopped thyme leaves
8 ounces pancetta, sliced thin
3 tablespoons olive oil
3 tablespoons butter
2 cups pomegranate juice
½ cup demi-glace

In a mixing bowl add the wild mushrooms, parsley, breadcrumbs, Parmesan and fontina cheese and egg. Mix well.

Clean pork tenderloin, butterfly and pound it thin, add the stuffing to the center and roll like a cigar. Rub the meat with salt, pepper, sage and thyme. Wrap the tenderloin with pancetta and tie with butcher string.

In a large sauté pan on high heat, add the oil and butter and brown tenderloin on all sides. Place in a 400 degree oven for 10 minutes. Remove from oven, remove the tenderloin from pan and deglaze with pomegranate juice. Reduce by half and add the demi-glace. Slice the tenderloin on a bias and serve over mashed potatoes. Top with pomegranate sauce.

6 servings

RANCHO CONTENTO CARNITAS

Patti Baker

This recipe is a crowd pleaser. You can serve them alone or with stuffed chilies as I do. The fruit salsa and Mango Sour Cream sauce are refreshing and complement the spicy carnitas.

1 8-pound pork butt roast
Salt and pepper
1 large sprig epazote
  (Mexican herb)
1 yellow onion, cut up
2 cloves garlic, sliced

2 oranges with skin, sliced
Low fat milk
Tortillas or gorditas
3 or 4 7-ounce cans
  (use your favorite salsa,
  hot, hotter or WOW!)

Put salt and pepper on outside of roast. Brown on all sides in a Dutch oven on top of the stove. When browned, remove from heat and drain any grease. Place epazote, onion, garlic and oranges on top and around the roast in the pot. Pour enough low-fat milk to cover ¾ of roast. Place a lid on Dutch oven and place in 300 degree oven for about 2 hours. Check to make sure there is enough liquid during this cooking time. Add more milk if needed.

After pork has cooked for 2 hours, add the salsa to the meat. You need enough moisture so the meat does not dry out. Cover and cook for 1 hour or more. Meat should start to fall apart. If you are going to use it the same day, allow meat to cool and shred apart, removing any extra fatty meat. If you are using it the next day, you can refrigerate in Dutch oven when meat has cooled. The next day, remove solidified fat and shred meat. Re-heat when ready to serve. This meat will last for several days in the refrigerator.

To serve: This dish is delicious with soft corn tortillas or gorditas, but you can use flour tortillas. Warm each tortilla on a cast iron skillet over high heat. Wrap in dish towel to keep warm. Serve carnitas on a platter or in a large serving bowl. Fill tortillas or gorditas with meat and add Mango-Papaya Salsa and Mango Sour Cream and eat like a taco.

MANGO-PAPAYA SALSA

1 mango, peeled, seeded and
  chopped
1 papaya, peeled, seeded and
  chopped
1 avocado, peeled, seeded and
  chopped

1 red onion, chopped
½ bunch cilantro
2 limes, juice only
Salt and pepper to taste

Chop the above ingredients and place in bowl with lime juice and salt and pepper.

MANGO SOUR CREAM SAUCE

1 small tub sour cream
1 mango, peeled and seeded

Dash of Tabasco sauce

Blend all ingredients in blender and refrigerate until ready to use. Use fresh cilantro and fresh squeezed lime for the top of each carnitas.

6 to 8 servings

GRILLED SUMMERTIME RIB-EYE

Pacific Connection Catering for Rodney Strong Vineyards

Suggested wine: 1998 Alden Vineyards Cabernet Sauvignon

8 cloves garlic
8 1-pound rib-eye steaks
Salt and pepper to taste
1 teaspoon chopped rosemary

1 teaspoon chopped oregano
2 yellow onions, sliced
4 portobello mushrooms

Cut the cloves of garlic into 3 pieces and insert them into the steaks. Sprinkle the steaks with salt and pepper and the chopped herbs. Sauté onions in a pan over medium heat until they slowly start to caramelize. Grill the steaks along with the portobello mushrooms. Remove the mushrooms and slice about ½-inch thick. Place the onion on the plate, top with the rib-eye, then the mushrooms. (You can remove the garlic if you prefer.)

8 servings

WINDSOR'S BEEF IN RED WINE SAUCE

Windsor Vineyards

1½ pound beef tenderloin
Salt and pepper
4 tablespoons butter, divided
4 large garlic cloves, chopped
3 large shallots, chopped

1 teaspoon dried thyme
1 tablespoon flour
2 cups beef broth
2 cups Windsor Merlot

Cut tenderloin into 12 equal rounds and pound them to a ¼-inch thickness. Season with salt and pepper. Melt 2 tablespoons butter over medium heat. Sauté beef in skillet until just pink in the center, then transfer to plate. Add remaining butter to the skillet, then add garlic, shallots and thyme; sauté until golden, about 3 minutes. Add flour, stir 1 minute. Add broth and wine. Boil until sauce thickens and is reduced to 1¼ cups, stirring occasionally. Return beef and juices to sauce in skillet. Heat through, about 1 minute. Transfer beef to plates, spoon sauce over.

4 servings

RACK OF LAMB WITH CILANTRO-MUSTARD SEED CRUST

Chef Phil McGauley, Kenwood Vineyards

1 tablespoon chopped cilantro
1 tablespoon Dijon mustard
1½ teaspoons mustard seeds
1 garlic clove, minced
1 pound rack of lamb, trimmed

1 teaspoon canola oil
Salt and pepper to taste
New Mexico Chili Sauce
   (recipe to follow)

Preheat oven to 450 degrees. In a small bowl mix together cilantro, mustard, mustard seeds and garlic and set aside. Season lamb with salt and pepper. Heat oil in ovenproof sauté pan over medium-high heat. Add lamb and brown on both sides. Remove from heat and spread mustard mixture over lamb. Transfer lamb to oven and roast to medium-rare, about 10 minutes. Serve with New Mexico Chili Sauce.

To serve, spoon half of the chili sauce on each plate, arrange lamb over sauce, garnish with confetti of diced peppers and parsley.

2 servings

NEW MEXICO CHILI SAUCE

Chef Phil McGauley, Kenwood Vineyards

2 plum tomatoes
2 dried New Mexico chilies,
  seeded and trimmed
1 tablespoon olive oil
1 small onion, chopped
2 cloves garlic, chopped

1 cup chopped shiitake
  mushrooms
½ teaspoon oregano
14 ounces chicken stock
1 teaspoon lemon juice
Pinch of sugar
Salt and pepper to taste

Roast tomatoes until blistering. Cool, peel and chop coarsely. In a small sauté pan, toast chilies over medium heat until fragrant. Let cool and tear into small pieces. In a medium sauté pan, heat oil over medium heat. Add onions, garlic and mushrooms and cook until soft. Add oregano and cook a little longer. Add chicken stock, tomatoes and chilies and bring to a boil. Reduce heat and simmer for about 20 minutes. Transfer sauce to a blender and purée. Strain into a saucepan and add lemon juice, sugar and season with salt and pepper.

Bodega Town

RED WINE MARINATED LAMB CHOPS

with Blue Lake Beans and Pomegranate

Chef Derek McCarthy, Tastings Restaurant and Wine Bar

2 racks of lamb
1 cup red wine
1 tablespoon chopped
   rosemary
1 tablespoon chopped parsley
4 tablespoons chopped garlic,
   divided
1 tablespoon chopped shallots

1 tablespoon juniper berries
56 blue lake beans
1 tablespoon chopped thyme
1 tablespoon olive oil
½ cup chicken stock
1 pomegranate, seeds removed
   (40 seeds reserved for
   garnish)

For Lamb: Clean racks of lamb into 16 chops. French the bones and marinate for 2 hours with red wine, rosemary, parsley, 3 tablespoons garlic, shallots and juniper berries. Season chops on one side with salt and pepper. Place on a hot grill 2 minutes per side.

For Beans: Clean beans and blanch in salted water for 1 to 2 minutes until al dente. In a large sauté pan, add 1 tablespoon garlic, beans, thyme and olive oil. Season with salt and pepper. Sauté until hot.

For Sauce: Pour marinade and ½ cup chicken stock with pomegranate seeds into a sauce pan. Bring to a boil and reduce until sauce coats backside of spoon. Strain through a fine strainer.

For Presentation: Place 7 beans in center of plate. Cross chops over beans. Drizzle sauce around plate and garnish with pomegranate seeds.

8 servings

Timber Crest Farms

Just out Dry Creek, past the grapevines and before you reach the lake, you'll find Timber Crest Farms. Sitting on a little knoll in the Dry Creek Valley of Sonoma County, Timber Crest Farms is about an hour and a half north of San Francisco, and 15 miles from the Pacific Ocean.

For more than 40 years the Waltenspiel family has farmed this fertile land. Together they plant, grow, harvest, dry and package organic and preservative-free dried fruits, nuts and tomatoes. No additives, no additude. Ronald and Ruth Waltenspiel say "The only thing we add is pride."

Stop by the farm if you are in the area. During the summer months they can show you dried fruit from the ground to the table.

4791 Dry Creek Road
Healdsburg, CA 95448
888-374-9325
www.timbercrest.com
rcf@timbercrest.com

Graziano's Ristorante

Graziano Perozzi's career as renowned chef began in Italy where, as a teenager, he attended hotel school, and progressed through a London club for the elite, and more studies in Sardinia, Cantebury and Switzerland. Next were night clubs in Bermuda and the Bahamas where he cooked for many famous people.

In 1969 he came to the U.S. and helped open a restaurant in Oakland, then to Guido's in San Rafael as head chef. Graziano said he chose to move to Petaluma because the area reminds him of his homeland in Italy. Graziano's Ristorante was opened 20 years ago and has become a landmark for authentic Italian food.

170 Petaluma Boulevard No.
Petaluma, CA 94952
(707) 762-5997

Spectrum Naturals/Spectrum Essentials

Jethren Phillips founded Spectrum Organic Products in 1981, the leader in organic and natural culinary and nutritional oils. We market Spectrum Naturals cooking oils, spreads, condiments and dressings, and Spectrum Essentials essential fatty acid (EFA) oils.

Jethren Phillips got into the business while in school, and left to open his own restaurant and bakery, offering only wholesome, high quality ingredients including expeller pressed unrefined oils. As the business grew, he continued to learn about the nutritional properties of oils.

There are a number of questions about oils. Why are some oils nutritious and others nutritionally bankrupt? Why is expeller pressing better for the environment? What does cold pressed mean? Why take flax oil?

If you have questions, come to Spectrum for the answer. Our web site is:

www.spectrumorganic.com

Angelo's Wine Country Deli

Angelo Ibleto is widely known in Sonoma County for the excellence of a sizable range of products he makes himself.

Topping the list is Angelo's smoked turkey, ham and bacon, a large number of smoked and fresh sausages, and eight kinds of beef jerky the San Francisco press said was "to die for."

Angelo also makes his own salsas, BBQ sauce, mustard, marinara sauce, and more, all available at his deli in the scenic Sonoma Valley.

23400 Arnold Drive
Sonoma, CA 95476
(707) 938-3688, FAX (707) 763-0841

e-mail: moregarlic@aol.com

Web: angelossmokehouse.com

Santa Rosa Meat and Poultry Co., Inc.

has been a family owned and operated meat and poultry distributor since 1982. Specializing in quality and service, this U.S.D.A. inspected, H.A.S.A.P. certified company offers a full line of the finest beef, pork, lamb and poultry products.

Santa Rosa Meat and Poultry Co., Inc., is Sonoma County's number one supplier of Fulton Valley Select Sonoma fryers. The business supplies many restaurants, meat shops, delicatessens and caterers in the greater North Bay. Make sure the food you serve has come from the place where quality and service are everything.

940 Ludwig Avenue
Santa Rosa, CA 95407
(707) 542-6234

Lombardi's Deli & Gourmet BBQ

Lee Lombardi celebrated the grand opening of Lombardi's Deli & Gourmet BBQ in Petaluma in 1999, and the rest, as they say, is history. The barbecues are hot all day cooking tri tips of beef, pork or beef ribs and chicken. The addition of a crab pot means fresh crab daily in season.

Fresh grilled vegetables, a gourmet salad, Lee's chili, baked beans and garlic bread, or a hot tri tip sandwich. Whether enjoyed at the deli or as take-out, the menu cannot be beat.

Lombardi's invites you to come by, pick up a rack of ribs, a whole or half chicken, plus a few sides on your way home and dinner is ready when you are.

Lombardi's also offers a wide selection of California wines and ice-cold beer, and is available for catering, with barbecue prepared on site.

Open 10-7, every day

3413 Petaluma Boulevard North
Petaluma, CA 94952
(707) 773-1271

139 Petaluma Boulevard North Downtown
Petaluma, CA 94952
(707) 763-6959

Santa Rosa Meat & Poultry Co.

Parkinson '02

SANTA ROSA MEAT & POULTRY CO.

Salt Point

SEAFOOD

COZZE E VONGOLE PEPERONATA

Mussels and Clams with Sweet Peppers

Chef Michael Ghilarducci, The Depot Hotel, Cucina Rustica

6 tablespoons olive oil
1 medium onion, peeled and
  sliced
1 large garlic clove, diced
4 bell peppers, 2 green and
  2 red, seeded, cored, and
  julienned
Salt and pepper
1½ cups skinned and chopped
  tomatoes
2 tablespoons red wine vinegar

1 tablespoon finely chopped
  parsley
20 2-inch fresh Manila or
  cherrystone clams, in the
  shell
20 fresh mussels, in the shell
2 tablespoons finely chopped
  shallots
2 cups white wine
Juice of 1 lemon

PEPERONATA

Heat the oil in a sauté pan, add the onion and garlic. Sauté for
5 minutes over medium heat until translucent. Add the bell
peppers, salt, and pepper to taste. Sauté 5 minutes longer,
stirring. Add the tomatoes, vinegar, and parsley and cover.
Simmer over low heat 30 minutes, until thickened.

SHELLFISH

To steam the shellfish separately, place ½ the shallots, ½ the
white wine, and the juice of ½ lemon in each of 2 medium
saucepans. Put the clams in one pan and the mussels in the
other and steam, covered, just until the shellfish opens. Remove
each pan from the fire just as soon as each type appears to be
open. Set aside and cool slightly.

ASSEMBLY

On each service plate put a mound of the peperonata sauce in
the center. Arrange the clams and mussels around the sauce,
alternating. Serve hot, chilled, or at room temperature.

4 servings

Depot Hotel — Sonoma

DEPOT HOTEL 1870

Parkinson '86

SAUTÉED SAND DABS WITH BLOOD ORANGES, FENNEL, AND ROCKET

Chef Mark Purdy, Dry Creek Kitchen

2 blood oranges, segmented
1 cup juice from the blood
  oranges
Extra virgin olive oil
2 pounds arugula, washed

1 head fennel, sliced thinly
6 whole sand dabs, filleted
3 tablespoons whole butter
Fresh thyme
Kosher salt and pepper to taste

Begin removing the rind from the oranges with a serrated knife. Remove each segment from the pith and set them aside. Squeeze the remaining juice out of the orange piths and reserve.

Make a vinaigrette with the orange juice by combining 1 part juice to 2 parts extra virgin olive oil. Season to taste and reserve.

Place the arugula and thinly sliced fennel in a mixing bowl and reserve for service.

Season the sand dab fillets with freshly ground pepper and kosher salt. Warm a heavy bottom skillet over medium heat. Add the butter and allow to foam in the pan, then add the sand dabs, skin side down. Cook gently over medium heat until the flesh begins to whiten around the edges of the flesh. Add the fresh thyme and baste the fish briefly, then remove from the pan and pat dry on a paper towel.

To serve, place a few orange segments on each of the service plates, creating a well for the salad. Add enough vinaigrette to the greens to coat them lightly, and season with salt and pepper. Place a handful of the dressed greens in the well created by the orange segments. Place 2 sand dab fillets atop the greens, and spoon some of the vinaigrette over the fish and around the plate. Serve immediately.

6 servings

WARM SEAFOOD SALAD

Emile Waldteufel, Creekside Bistro

⅓ cup water or white wine
3 cloves garlic, minced,
   divided
Juice of ¼ lemon
1½ ounces butter, divided
12 Manila clams
4 scallops
4 prawns
1 4-ounce salmon filet cut into
   4 pieces
2 tablespoons fresh white corn

2 tablespoons diced beets
2 tablespoons diced tomatoes
⅓ cup balsamic vinegar
⅛ cup olive oil
4 ounces bay shrimp
⅓ cup finely chopped parsley
Salt and pepper
A mix of red leaf lettuce and
   butter lettuce
Fine julienne of red onion

Place a mixing bowl over a pot of hot water to keep the bowl warm during the cooking and assembly of the salad. Begin by bringing to a boil water or white wine, 1 clove minced garlic, lemon juice and ½ ounce butter. Add clams and steam covered with a lid. Pour clams and juice into the mixing bowl.

Lightly flour scallops, prawns and salmon and sauté in a hot, oiled pan. Do not overcook. Remove seafood from pan to mixing bowl and discard the hot oil. Add remaining butter and brown lightly. Add remaining garlic, corn, beets and tomatoes. Shake pan, add balsamic vinegar and bring to a boil. Remove from heat and add olive oil, bay shrimp and parsley. Add salt and fresh ground pepper to taste. Add to mixing bowl. Stir ingredients together.

To assemble, mix lettuces and onion and place a handful in the center of each plate. Surround with equal parts of seafood. Pour dressing over seafood and lettuces and serve with crusty French bread.

2 as entrée or 4 as appetizer

PRAWNS SANTORINI

Chef Christine Topolos, Russian River Vineyards

This dish is named for the island of Santorini, so long under Italian rule that the name stayed with the dish even after the island reverted to Greek control and its Greek name, Thira

¼ cup kalamata olive oil
20-28 medium prawns, peeled
  and deveined
1 cup minced green onion
  (cut rings ⅛-inch thick)
2 cups chopped tomato meat

1 cup cubed feta cheese
  (½-inch cubes)
1½ tablespoons fresh minced
  dill
½ cup dry white wine
  (Chardonnay or Sauvignon
  Blanc)

Warm the olive oil over medium heat in a sauté pan broad enough to hold all of the prawns in a single layer. Fill the pan with the prawns, turn each prawn over when the underside has lost its raw appearance (only 1 or 2 minutes). Add the green onion; if there is room, try to get the onion on the pan surface, not just on top of the prawns. Sauté 1 minute more and then add all the other ingredients. Raise the heat to high and cover with a closely fitting lid. Simmer 3 minutes, stir and serve over rice. So fast and so easy you can do it while your guests look on in awe and admiration.

4 servings

MARINATED GRILLED SWORDFISH

Chef Laurie Souza, Korbel Champagne Cellars

¼ cup white wine vinegar
1 cup olive oil
2 lemons, juiced
¼ cup capers, drained and
   rinsed
½ cup water
4 cloves garlic, minced

Salt and freshly ground white
   pepper to taste
6 roma tomatoes
8 ½-inch thick swordfish
   steaks (about 4 pounds)
1 cup basil leaves, julienned

In a bowl, combine the white wine vinegar, olive oil, lemon
juice, water and garlic. Season with salt and pepper. Set aside.
Cut the tomatoes into quarters, seed and dice them and reserve.
Preheat grill or barbecue. Brush the fish lightly with the marinade and put it on the grill. Cook approximately 2 minutes per
side. Place the fish in a dish large enough to hold one layer. Mix
the remaining marinade with ½ cup of the basil leaves and the
diced tomatoes. Pour over the swordfish and marinate for about
1 hour at room temperature. Garnish with the remainder of basil
before serving.

8 servings

Sundown Surf

BOLINHO DE BACALHAU

Baked Cod Cakes Served with Cilantro Mayonnaise, Sliced Egg and Mixed Greens

Chef Manuel Azevedo, LaSalette Restaurant

½ pound dried salt cod
2 medium russet potatoes
1 small yellow onion, minced
2 garlic cloves, minced
1 tablespoon parsley, minced
1 large egg
1 pinch each of nutmeg,
  cayenne and white pepper
½ cup corn flour

2 tablespoons olive oil
1 tablespoon cilantro, minced
1 cup mayonnaise
Mixed greens
Oil and vinegar
6 hard-boiled eggs
Mixed greens
Portuguese olives for garnish

Soak cod for 24 hours. Change water several times. Boil cod until tender, 5 to 10 minutes depending on thickness. Chill. Boil, peel and chill potatoes. Sauté onion and garlic until soft and chill.

Shred cod and potatoes with a fork or beat with the paddle attachment of a kitchen mixer. Combine shredded cod and potatoes with onion, garlic, parsley, egg, nutmeg and peppers by hand in a mixing bowl. Knead mixture until balls can be formed. Taste for salt and pepper. Make individual 2-ounce balls, egg shaped, and roll in corn flour.

In a large nonstick sauté pan, heat olive oil and brown cod cakes, turning several times. Bake in a 375 degree preheated oven for 15 minutes.

Combine cilantro and mayonnaise. Toss mixed greens with oil and vinegar. On a chilled plate, serve hot cod cakes along-side the cilantro mayonnaise. Garnish with mixed greens, sliced egg and olives.

6 servings

GLAZED SEA BASS
WITH GINGER BUTTER SAUCE

Chef Phil McGauley, Korbel Champagne Cellars

1 cup white wine	3 teaspoons rice wine vinegar
⅓ cup chopped shallots	1½ teaspoons cold water
⅓ cup thinly sliced ginger	1½ teaspoons cornstarch
½ cup heavy cream	4 6-ounce sea bass fillets
6 tablespoons soy sauce	4 tablespoons butter
3 tablespoons honey	

Combine wine, shallots and ginger in small sauce pan over high heat. Boil until liquid is reduced to ¼ cup. Add cream and boil liquid until reduced by half. Remove from heat.

Mix soy sauce, honey and rice wine vinegar in another small sauce pan. Mix water and cornstarch in a small bowl until smooth. Add to soy sauce mixture. Stir over medium heat until glaze boils and thickens slightly. Remove from heat and cool to room temperature. Preheat oven to 350 degrees. Arrange fish on small sheet pan. Brush with some glaze. Bake until opaque in center. Remove from oven. Bring sauce to a simmer, gradually add butter to sauce, whisking just until melted. Strain. Season with salt and pepper. Spoon sauce onto 4 plates, dividing equally. Top with fish and serve.

4 servings

PRAWNS BORDELAISE

Chef, Roger Praplan, LaGare French Restaurant

8 prawns - under 15 in size
Flour
1 egg (for egg wash)
2 tablespoons oil
Salt and white pepper
½ teaspoon diced shallots

½ teaspoon diced garlic
4 ounces butter
¼ teaspoon lemon juice
1 teaspoon chopped parsley
½ cup white wine

Devein prawns and butterfly through the back. Dust with flour and dip in the egg wash. Heat the oil in a skillet. When hot (not smoking), lay prawns flat and brown them. Season with salt and white pepper. Turn prawns over, drain the oil and add shallots, garlic, butter, lemon juice, parsley and finally the white wine. Let the sauce thicken. If sauce breaks, add a little more white wine to bring it back to proper consistency.

Serve with Pedroncelli Rosé

2 servings

SHRIMP CAKES

Chef Robert Buchshachermaier, Café Europe

2 medium baking potatoes,
    peeled and quartered
½ cup butter, divided
1½ cups Cheddar cheese,
    grated
1 egg yolk
3 tablespoons chopped parsley

1 medium onion, finely
    chopped
1 pound cooked shelled
    shrimp, chopped
Flour
Beaten egg
Breadcrumbs

Boil the potatoes in salted water until they are fork soft. Drain and mash with a fork. Add ⅔ of the butter, cheese, yolk, parsley and mix well until the mixture is smooth. Melt the remaining butter in a frying pan. Add the onions and cook for 5 minutes. Add the shrimp and cook for 1 minute. Add the shrimp to the potatoes and mix together well. Form into round shapes, approximately 1½-inch in diameter. Roll in flour, drop in egg, cover with breadcrumbs and put cakes on waxed paper. Deep fry, turning them over when they are golden. Serve hot or cold.

SEARED SEA SCALLOPS
WITH SAFFRON NAGE

Chef Elizabeth A. Ozanich, Brasserie de la Mer

16 ounces U-10 dry-pack sea
  scallops
Oil for frying
4 ounces truffle infused
  unsalted butter (see below)
4 ounces leeks cooked in
  butter
16 ounces fingerling potatoes
  cooked and peeled

Salt and pepper
2 ounces truffle oil
16 ounces Saffron Cream
  Sauce (see below)
8 ounces assorted cherry
  tomatoes
1 tablespoon fresh chervil

Season scallops with salt and pepper. Preheat a sauté pan with oil and get it very hot. Place scallops in pan being careful not to splash oil. Sear scallops until golden but medium rare. In a separate pan melt truffle butter. Add leeks and potatoes and sauté until heated through. Season with salt and pepper and finish with truffle oil. Pour fat from scallop pan. Set scallops aside and keep warm. Heat saffron cream and cherry tomatoes in scallop pan.

In a deep soup plate, place potatoes in center, pour in saffron sauce and arrange scallops around. Garnish with chervil leaves.

SAFFRON CREAM SAUCE
1 cup white wine
1 teaspoon saffron threads

1 quart heavy cream

Reduce 1 cup white wine by half and add 1 teaspoon saffron threads. Reduce 1 quart of cream by half and add wine reduction. Sauce should be thick enough to coat back of spoon.

TRUFFLE BUTTER
1/4 teaspoon truffle

4 ounces unsalted butter

Shave fresh truffle or use canned truffle and fold into butter. Allow it to infuse for 24 hours.

4 servings

SHRIMP WITH GINGER-GRILLED PINEAPPLE

Chef Phil McGauley, Korbel Champagne Cellars

1 teaspoon olive oil
12 large shrimp, shelled and
  deveined
Salt and pepper
1 small onion, diced
½ teaspoon minced garlic
½ cup orange juice
¼ cup lime juice, divided

2 tablespoons minced green
  onions
2 tablespoons chopped cilantro
1 tablespoon plus 1 teaspoon
  minced fresh ginger
1 tablespoon sesame oil
1 pineapple, peeled, cored and
  quartered
1 teaspoon sesame seeds

Heat oil in large sauté pan. Season the shrimp with salt and pepper and cook over high heat. Add onion and garlic and cook, stirring occasionally, until shrimp are cooked through. Stir in orange juice, 2 tablespoons lime juice with the green onions, cilantro, ginger, sesame oil, ½ teaspoon salt and ¼ teaspoon pepper. Brush the pineapple with mixture and let set for 30 minutes. Toast the sesame seeds until lightly brown. Grill the pineapple until lightly brown. Cut each quarter crosswise into 6 pieces and arrange on 6 plates. Set 2 shrimp on each plate, spoon a little orange juice marinade and sprinkle with sesame seeds.

6 servings

BAKED OYSTERS ITALIANO

Chef Tess Ostopowicz, GTO's Seafood House

3 dozen oysters
½ stick butter, melted
½ cup olive oil
1 lemon, juice only
2 teaspoons Worcestershire
  sauce

1 clove garlic, minced
2 tablespoons vermouth or dry
  white wine
1 cup breadcrumbs, seasoned
¾ cup grated Parmesan cheese
⅔ cup minced parsley

Drain oysters well on paper towels. Combine butter, olive oil, lemon juice, Worcestershire sauce, garlic and wine. Mix breadcrumbs, parsley and cheese. In a casserole, make layers of oysters, the butter-oil, liquids and finally the crumb-cheese mixture. Bake in a 450 degree oven until the oyster edges begin to curl (about 10 to 12 minutes). Remove and serve immediately.

4 to 6 servings

KASU SAKE SALMON

Chef Jesse McQuarrie, Feast an American Bistro

This dish gives you an opportunity to use some ingredients that might be new to you, but that are readily available. At my restaurant, I always put this dish on the menu when salmon season opens on the Sonoma Coast.

Kasu is the left over yeast fermentation at the bottom of the sake barrels. You can find or order it at Asian markets. Furikake is a Japanese spice mix, also available at Asian markets.

1 3-pound salmon filet

KASU MARINADE
¾ cup mirin
¼ cup rice vinegar
½ cup sugar

¾ cup light soy sauce
1½ cups kasu
Kosher salt

Set oven to broil. Heat all of ingredients together except the kasu. Pour into a blender, add kasu and blend together until well incorporated. Let cool. Spread a liberal layer of marinade over the salmon and season with kosher salt. Broil in oven for 10 to 12 minutes. Salmon should be slightly caramelized, with the kasu giving it a teriyaki type of look. Serve with steamed spinach, grated daikon radish, Meyer lemon wedges, and Sweet Shoyu Sauce (recipe follows).

4 to 8 servings

SWEET SHOYU SAUCE

Chef Jesse McQuarrie, Feast an American Bistro

3 cups water
3 cups rice vinegar
2 cups light soy sauce
   (preferably Kikkoman's)
2 cups sugar

2 tablespoons Ebi furikake
¼ cup white truffle oil
3 tablespoons cornstarch
3 tablespoons water

Combine first 6 ingredients in a non-reactive pan and bring to a boil. Mix cornstarch and 3 tablespoons water together and add to boiling sauce. Stir with a whisk for 1 minute. Turn off heat. The sauce should coat the back of a spoon.

NUT CRUSTED HALIBUT

Chef Randy Hoppe, Catelli's The Rex

4 halibut fillets, 6 to 7 ounces
¼ cup flour
2 eggs
3 tablespoons milk

1 teaspoon grated fresh ginger
½ cup pecans, minced
½ cup pine nuts, minced

Preheat oven to 400 degrees. Flour top of halibut fillet. Beat together eggs and milk and dip top of fillet in egg wash. Combine ginger and nuts and coat halibut top with mixture. Heat sauté pan over medium heat, add oil and sauté with nut crust down until nuts begin to brown (being careful not to burn) for 1 to 2 minutes. Turn fillets over and place in oven for 6 to 8 minutes (2 to 3 minutes longer for thick fillets). Serve with Roasted Red Bell Pepper Sauce (recipe follows).

4 servings

ROASTED RED BELL PEPPER SAUCE

Chef Randy Hoppe, Catelli's The Rex

2 red bell peppers
2 tablespoons olive oil
4 cloves garlic, peeled

¾ cup chicken stock
½ cup heavy cream
Salt and pepper to taste

Heat oven to 400 degrees. Cut peppers in half, rub with olive oil and place in pan with cut side down. Roast in oven until peppers are darkened, but not completely black. Remove from oven and place in closed paper bag for 10 minutes. Remove from bag and peel skin, seeds and veins from peppers. Add garlic and peppers to food processor and purée. Add chicken stock and blend. Pour into saucepan and add cream. Simmer until thickened. Add salt and pepper to taste.

SHRIMP CREOLE

Chef Tess Ostopowicz, GTO's Seafood House

1 cup flour
1 cup vegetable oil
2 cups chopped onions, red or
  yellow, or 1 cup each
1 cup chopped celery
½ cup bell pepper, green or a
  combination of colors
2 cloves chopped garlic
1 large can tomatoes or 4 large
  tomatoes, about 2 pounds,
  peeled
2 small cans tomato paste
3 teaspoons salt

¼ teaspoon cayenne pepper
½ teaspoon fresh ground black
  pepper
6 cups water or stock (shrimp,
  vegetable or chicken)
3 pounds raw deveined shrimp
2 tablespoons chopped parsley
2 tablespoons chopped green
  onion, white and tender
  green parts
Chopped green onion for
  garnish

Make a roux of flour and vegetable oil. Brown over slow fire, stirring constantly, to the color of peanut butter. Add onion, celery, bell pepper and garlic. Cook until soft. Add tomatoes and tomato paste and seasonings except parsley and green onions. Cook about 5 minutes, then add water or stock. Let simmer about 1 hour. Add shrimp, parsley and onion tops 5 minutes before serving. Serve over white or brown rice. Garnish with green onions.

About 10 servings

BAKED SALMON WITH
ALL RED OR CRANBERRY POTATOES

Oh! Tommy Boy's Organic Farm

1 filet salmon
Juice of 1 lemon
1 pinch of rosemary

3 bay leaves
3 medium All Red or
  Cranberry potatoes

Preheat oven to 325 degrees. Place salmon on flat baking sheet and squeeze lemon juice over fish. Sprinkle with rosemary. Put bay leaves on fish. Slice potatoes and put around fish. Bake for 30 minutes or until done.

PESTO CRUSHED SALMON
WITH TOMATO BELL PEPPER RELISH

Andy's Produce Market, Katie Heing, Andy's Granddaughter

This recipe is great hot or cold, and is very easy to prepare.

SALMON

4 salmon steaks   Salt and pepper
1 cup pesto (Andy's brand)

Rinse salmon, pat dry. Season both sides with salt and pepper.
Heat in a large frying pan on medium heat. Using ¼ cup pesto,
coat both sides of each salmon steak, gently place in pan. Cook
approximately 5 to 6 minutes on each side. While salmon is
cooking, make the relish.

RELISH

½ cup each red, orange, yellow   2 tablespoons olive oil
    and green bell pepper   3 tablespoons balsamic vinegar
1 teaspoon chopped garlic   ¼ cup chopped fresh basil
1 teaspoon salt   leaves (12 to 14)
¼ teaspoon pepper   1 cup fresh chopped tomatoes

Stir-fry bell peppers and garlic on high heat 1 to 2 minutes,
remove from heat. Add remaining ingredients and toss well.
Spoon ¼ cup relish on each salmon steak. Serve with wild rice,
red-skinned mashed potatoes or pasta.

4 servings

DUNGENESS CRAB SPRING ROLLS WITH GAZPACHO DIPPING SAUCE

Chef Gary Arthur, Terrace Grill at Flamingo Resort Hotel

1 pound crabmeat	1 inch fresh ginger, julienned
3 green onions, chopped	and fried
4 large basil leaves, chopped	1 kaffir lime leaf
1 sweet red pepper, chopped	1 cup shredded fresh coconut
4 cloves roasted garlic,	1 cup white breadcrumbs
chopped	1 tablespoon curry paste
	12 spring roll wraps

Simply mix all ingredients except spring roll wraps together over medium heat. Do not drain the crabmeat. Using small pieces of plastic wrap, roll 1½ tablespoon portions firmly together. Finally, roll into spring roll wraps, sealing the ends with flour and water paste. Fry in light oil, turning frequently. Drain on a clean paper towel.

GAZPACHO DIPPING SAUCE

1 cup V8 juice	2 tablespoons olive oil
½ stick celery	1 tablespoon red wine vinegar
1 clove garlic	1 teaspoon sugar
¼ red onion	1 small spicy pepper
1 sprig basil	Juice of 1 lime
1 sprig oregano	

Combine all ingredients and bring to a quick boil. Blend to purée. Chill for 1 hour. Strain if desired.

Notes: You will need to visit the Asian section of your local market for some ingredients.

Shelf life for rolls is 2 days stored at 40 degrees Fahrenheit.

Shelf life for sauce is 5 days stored at 40 degrees Fahrenheit.

6 to 8 servings

PAN SEARED HALIBUT

with English Peas, Fava Beans,
Olive Oil Mashed Potatoes and Artichoke Salad

Chef Jesse Mallgren, Madrona Manor

This recipe is made in four different parts.

1. *Artichoke salad where the artichokes are raw, but cooked in lemon juice.*

2. *Olive oil mashed potatoes, replacing some of the butter with olive oil to reduce the fat and provide a healthier dish.*

3. *Spring vegetables in an herbed vegetable stock broth.*

4. *Cooking of the halibut*

You will need to start with the artichoke salad because the artichokes need to marinate for at least 1 hour; they will remain fine for at least 4 hours.

ARTICHOKE SALAD

2 large artichokes
2 large lemons
2 shallots, sliced paper thin on a mandolin

½ cup Italian parsley, washed and stems removed
1 tablespoon extra virgin olive oil

Remove tough outer leaves and stems from the artichokes so only the heart remains, making sure any green is trimmed away. Cut artichoke heart in half and remove the choke with a spoon. Rub artichokes with a lemon to prevent discoloration. Slice artichokes paper thin on a mandolin. Mix with sliced shallots, parsley and juice from 1 lemon. Let artichokes sit for 1 hour.

OLIVE OIL MASHED POTATOES

2 large Yukon gold potatoes, peeled and cut into ¼-inch pieces
½ cup milk

¼ cup extra virgin olive oil
2 ounces butter
Salt and pepper to taste

Cook potatoes in salted water until tender. Drain potatoes well or the mashed potatoes will become mushy and less flavorful. Put the potatoes through a food mill or a ricer. Warm milk, olive oil and butter and stir into potatoes, making sure not to over-mix or the potatoes will become gummy. Season to taste. Set aside in a warm place until ready to serve.

SPRING VEGETABLE RAGOÛT

2 pounds fresh fava beans	½ cup canola oil
1 pound English peas	1 cup vegetable stock
1 bunch basil leaves, stems	2 tablespoons butter
removed	Salt and pepper to taste

Shell fresh fava beans from their pods. Quickly blanch beans in salted water, refreshing in ice bath. Remove outer skin leaving only the inside bean. Shell English peas, quickly blanch in salted water and refresh in ice bath. Blanch basil leaves in boiling salted water for 15 seconds, immediately refresh in ice water. Squeeze excess water out of basil and chop roughly. Blend basil and canola oil in blender on high for 2 minutes, strain off oil. (You can use this oil in a salad or to flavor vegetables at a later time). Refrigerate puréed basil. As you are cooking fish, heat the vegetable stock with the peas and fava beans. When the mixture comes to a boil, turn down the heat and add butter. Just before serving add 2 tablespoons of the basil purée.

HALIBUT

6 halibut filets, skin and bones	2 tablespoons canola oil
removed	Salt and pepper

After the artichokes, mashed potatoes and vegetable ragoût are finished you are ready to cook the fish. Season both sides of the fish with salt and pepper. In a non-stick pan, heat the canola oil until it starts to smoke. Add the halibut and cook on high for 30 seconds, then turn the heat down to medium. This will ensure that the fish develops a nice crust without burning. After 3 minutes turn the fish over and cook on the other side for 3 minutes.

Divide vegetable ragoût among four bowls, place approximately ½ cup of mashed potatoes in the center of the bowl, place the fish on top of the mashed potatoes and top the fish with the artichoke salad.

4 servings

OYSTER STEW

Chef Carlo Galazzo, Tides Wharf Restaurant

8 freshly opened oysters
2 tablespoons butter, divided
¼ cup oyster liquor
Dash celery salt

1 teaspoon Worcestershire
 sauce
1 ounce sherry
½ teaspoon paprika
1 cup half-and-half

Place all ingredients, except half-and-half and 1 tablespoon of the butter, into the top part of a double boiler over boiling water. Do not let the top pan touch the water. Whisk or stir briskly and constantly for about 1 minute, until oysters are just beginning to curl. Add half-and-half and continue stirring, briskly, just to a boil but don't boil.

Pour stew into a soup plate. Serve piping hot topped with the remaining 1 tablespoon of butter and sprinkle with paprika.

1 serving

BAGNA CALDA

Gina Gallo, Gallo of Sonoma

2½-3 cups olive oil
10 ounces peeled garlic, sliced
 thin, more if wanted
7 ounces drained anchovies
 (Spanish)

2-3 cubes butter
 (use unsalted butter for
 low-salt bagna)

Put olive oil and garlic in a heavy pot and cook at very low heat, stirring with a wooden spoon until the garlic is cooked. (Garlic should keep its white color and is completely cooked when it becomes very, very soft and can melt into a paste when pressed against the wall of the pot with the spoon). Add the anchovies to the above mixture and keep stirring until they melt into a paste of heavy sauce. Add the butter and keep stirring until all butter is melted.

The Bagna Calda is now ready to eat. Keep the pot at a very low heat and keep stirring all the time while eating. Suggested vegetables for dipping are bell pepper (roasted or raw), Napa cabbage, cardoni, cauliflower (parboiled), Jerusalem artichokes, leeks (parboiled), mushrooms.

About 8 servings

TROPICAL TANTRUM

Chef Robert Steiner, DeSchmire Restaurant

SEARED AHI STEAK WITH PACIFIC THAI SALSA

4 6-ounce #1 sushi quality ahi steaks, 1-inch thick	8 baby carrots, parboiled 4 minutes
	16 snow peas, parboiled 2 minutes

GARNISH

1 Belgian endive	1 lime, sliced
1 lemon, sliced	1 red and 1 yellow beet (optional)

SALSA

Several sprigs of fresh basil and pineapple sage	1 piece lemon grass
	1 lemon, juice only
Several leaves of fresh mint	1 teaspoon sesame oil
½ bunch cilantro	1 teaspoon olive oil
4 slices fresh ginger	¼ cup tropical fruit juice
2 cloves garlic	Salt and pepper to taste
2 jalapeño peppers - seeds removed	1 tomato, chopped
	1 roasted red pepper, chopped
2 tablespoons capers and juice	

Place all salsa ingredients except tomato and red pepper into a blender. Blend off and on for several spins. Then add tomato and red pepper. Sear ahi for 1 minute on each side. When done, place in center of plate. Fill individual endive leaves with salsa and arrange on each side of ahi steak. Arrange peas and carrots. Add lime and lemon slices. Put beets through Japanese turning slicer and decorate plate.

4 servings

CARAMEL PRAWNS

Jan Rosen, Executive Chef, J.M. Rosen's Waterfront Grill

6 large prawns	2 tablespoons brown sugar
1 teaspoon oil	2 tablespoons unsalted butter
1 cup orange juice	

Sauté prawns in hot oil. Turn when brown or starting to curl slightly. Add orange juice and brown sugar and reduce. Take prawns out of pan, add butter and reduce until caramelized.

1 serving

BOUILLABAISSE

Chef Patrick Martin, Charcuterie

4 pounds monkfish fillets, trimmed	2 tablespoons extra virgin olive oil
4 pounds rock cod fillets, boned	½ tablespoon saffron
	Fennel tops chopped
3 pounds John Dory (or Porgy)	2 tablespoons chopped garlic

Six hours before serving marinate the fish fillets in olive oil, saffron, fennel tops and garlic.

ROUILLE

2 cups good fish stock	Salt and cayenne pepper to taste
1 monkfish liver (optional)	
2 egg yolks	¾ cup olive oil
1 tablespoon Dijon mustard	1 cup breadcrumbs
1 tablespoon chopped garlic	

Poach monkfish liver in boiling fish stock for 2 to 3 minutes. At the restaurant I poach the liver when the soup is cooking using a "spider". Make aïoli using the egg Dijon mustard, garlic, salt, cayenne and olive oil. Add chopped monkfish liver. Thicken mixture with breadcrumbs.

FISH SOUP

2 yellow onions, sliced thin	6 tomatoes, peeled, seeded and chopped
2 medium leeks, sliced	
2 pounds carrots, sliced	7½ quarts good fish stock
2 bulbs fresh fennel, tops chopped (for rouille), bulbs julienne	12 medium potatoes, quartered
	3 pounds PEI mussels, cleaned
1¾ cups chopped garlic	12 slices toasted French bread (crouton)
1½ tablespoons good Spanish saffron	

Sauté onions, leek, carrots, fennel, garlic, saffron and tomatoes. Add fish stock, bring to boil and simmer for 45 minutes. Add potatoes, cooking 30 minutes more. Add mussels, then 10 minutes later the marinated fish, starting with the thickest fish and adding the thinnest last. Cook until fish are done.

TO SERVE

Spread crouton with Rouille, place poached fish and mussels in bowl, ladling broth and vegetables over top with crouton.

12 servings

Restaurant Charcuterie – Heilsburg

Restaurant Charcuterie

Mulhouse '96

HONEY GLAZED SALMON
WITH APPLE-WATERCRESS SALAD

Phil McGauley, Korbel Champagne Cellars

HONEY GLAZED SALMON

Juice of 4 limes
¼ cup honey
2 tablespoons mustard
Salt and pepper to taste
4 salmon filets, skinned and
    deboned

1 bunch fresh thyme
1 cup fish stock
½ cup Korbel Chardonnay
    Champagne

APPLE-WATERCRESS SALAD

2 Belgian endive
2 Granny Smith apples
1 tablespoon whole grain
    mustard
1 tablespoon honey

1 tablespoon rice wine vinegar
1 tablespoon olive oil
Salt and pepper to taste
4 bunches watercress, washed
    and stemmed

In a shallow baking dish, mix together lime juice, honey, mustard, and salt and pepper to taste. Add salmon and let marinate for 20 minutes. Preheat oven to 400 degrees. Spread the thyme on the bottom of the baking pan. Place the salmon on top. Add stock and champagne. Cook salmon until medium rare. Remove from oven, leave salmon in liquid.

Quarter 2 heads of endive. Slice thin wedges of apple, discarding the core. In a large bowl, mix mustard, honey, vinegar, olive oil, and salt and pepper to taste. Add the endive, watercress and apple slices. Mix well. Divide the salad onto 4 plates. Place a piece of salmon on each salad.

4 servings

Gallo Family's

GALLO *of* SONOMA.

The Gallo family vineyards and winery in Sonoma County produce internationally renowned wines under the direction of a third generation Gallo winemaker.

The vineyards lie across some of the most famous and prestigious growing regions of California: the Dry Creek Valley, Alexander Valley, Russian River Valley, and Sonoma Coast. Careful farming practices developed over many years are based on deeply held beliefs in conservation, preservation, and reliance on the land to serve the grandchildren and great grandchildren of the winery founders.

The diverse climate and terrain of Sonoma County allow Gallo of Sonoma winegrowers to match sites with vines to produce varietal wines that are true to the grape as well as to the land. The Gallo of Sonoma winemaking philosophy requires that Nature leads the process both in the vineyard and in the winery.

The Gallo of Sonoma Tasting Room on Healdsburg's historic downtown Plaza invites wine lovers to sample some of the special reserve and limited production wines that are available only there and in local Sonoma County restaurants.

Other wines from Gallo of Sonoma, such as the much sought-after Northern Sonoma Estate cabernet sauvignon and chardonnay, the site-specific vineyard-designated bottlings, and the Sonoma County appellated wines can be found in fine wine shops and restaurants around the world.

Gallo of Sonoma Tasting Room
320 Center Street
Healdsburg, CA 95448
Telephone: (707) 433-2548

Vineyard Creek

Parkerson '03

Vineyard Creek Hotel, Spa & Conference Center

In 2002, Sonoma County's long-awaited new Vineyard Creek Hotel, Spa and Conference Center opened in the historic section of Santa Rosa. Centrally situated within easy reach of 200 wineries, this dramatic new facility offers Sonoma County a much-needed major conference facility, and more.

The style of Vineyard Creek, according to The Connoisseurs Guide to the World's Best Resorts & Great Hotels, "evokes a Mediterranean village. Hidden courtyards and high stucco walls create a sense of privacy amid the richly detailed appointments and landscaping."

The hotel's restaurant is Brasserie de la Mer, created by James Beard award-winning chef Phillippe Boulot. The menu features classic French country fare based on Sonoma County products and the finest and freshest area seafood.

Next door is Santa Rosa's famed Railroad Square, a collection of fine old buildings and sought-after shops and award-winning restaurants - a destination in itself.

The hotel, with its 155 rooms, offers a dazzling array of guest services, including voice mail, complimentary newspapers and polished shoes, complimentary high speed internet access, 24-hour room service, robes, hair dryers, and much more.

The conference center offers 15,000 square feet of outdoor event space and 21,000 square feet of indoor meeting space. The Grand Ballroom can accommodate groups up to 1,000. Staff planners are available to help groups with special spa packages and wine country tours.

And that's not all. Guests also have access to massage, facials, aromatherapy, manicures, waxing, and full body treatment. Don't miss the ultimate wine country experience - grape-herbal elixir and grape-seed oil exfoliation.

In addition to wineries, Vineyard Creek is also an easy drive to the Charles M. Schulz Museum, Safari West Wild Animal Park, and the ruggedly scenic Pacific coast.

170 Railroad Street
Santa Rosa, CA 95401
(707) 636-7100
FAX 636-7277

Salt Point

PASTA

RANCHER'S PASTA

Timbercrest Farms

12-16 ounces dried or fresh fettuccine, cooked, drained and kept warm
1½ ounces (half a 3-ounce package) Sonoma Dried Tomato halves
1 tablespoon olive oil

4 cloves garlic, minced or pressed
1 cup pitted and halved or sliced black olives
1 teaspoon crushed oregano
8 ounces crumbled feta cheese or grated mozzarella cheese

Soften tomato halves by placing in a heatproof bowl. Pour a quantity of boiling water over the tomatoes to cover. Let sit 5 minutes. Drain and slice tomato halves into strips. Heat oil in a large skillet. Add garlic to skillet and sauté 2 minutes over medium heat. Add olives, tomatoes and oregano and cook 2 more minutes. Add cheese, stir and remove from heat. Pour sauce over pasta and toss to blend thoroughly. Serve immediately.

2 servings

FIDEOS CON POLLO Y CHAMPIGNONES

Egg Noodles with Chicken and Mushrooms, Peruvian Style

Patty Karlin, Bodega Goat Cheese

1 cup fresh mushrooms (portabello or brown field)
½ cup butter, divided
2 tablespoons flour
1 can evaporated goat's milk (Meyenberg)
Salt and pepper

2 eggs, beaten
1 cup dry sherry
3 chicken breasts, chopped in small pieces and cooked
1 cup Queso Cabrero, grated, divided
1 pound egg noodles, cooked

Cut the mushrooms in strips, dry them well and sauté in 1 tablespoon butter for 3 minutes. Remove from pan and set aside. Melt the rest of the butter and stir in flour, then the milk, salt and pepper. Simmer for 1 minute. Remove from heat and add the eggs, sherry, chopped chicken breast, mushrooms and half of the cheese. Place half the noodles in a greased Pyrex baking dish, put the sauce on top, add more noodles, then sprinkle with remaining cheese. Bake in 350 degree oven until golden on top, being careful not to let it dry out.

6 servings

SMOKED QUAIL PASTA WITH SPINACH, SUN-DRIED TOMATOES AND WALNUTS

Chef Laurie Souza, Korbel Champagne Cellars

1 pound penne pasta
5 quail, smoked and deboned
1 bunch spinach
1 cup sun-dried tomatoes in oil
2 ounces radicchio, sliced into thin strips
1 eggplant, sliced into rounds

Olive oil
Salt and freshly ground black pepper
1 cup oil-cured black olives
1 cup walnuts, toasted and chopped
1½ cups Parmesan cheese

VINAIGRETTE

2 tablespoons balsamic vinegar
1 teaspoon sherry vinegar

Sun-dried tomato oil plus walnut oil to make ½ cup total
Salt and black pepper to taste

Boil pasta in salted water for 8 minutes. Drain and refresh. Remove meat from smoked quail and shred. Remove stems from spinach and slice into thin strips (chiffonade). Drain sun-dried tomatoes and reserve oil. Julienne the tomatoes. Brush the eggplant with olive oil. Season with salt and pepper. Grill or sauté until golden. Cool and dice. Cut the black olives into slivers. Combine the pasta with the meat, tomatoes, eggplant, olives and walnuts.

Combine the two vinegars in a small bowl. Slowly add the oil while whisking to emulsify the dressing. Season with salt and freshly ground black pepper.

If you would like to serve this pasta at room temperature, you can add the vinaigrette now along with the spinach, radicchio and cheese. If you prefer the dish hot/warm, place the pasta in a glass bowl and cover with plastic wrap. Microwave on high for 3 to 4 minutes. Add the spinach, radicchio and cheese. Garnish with additional cheese if desired.

8 servings

GNOCCHI AL MASCARPONE E PARMIGIANO

Chef Luca Citti, Cafe Citti

GNOCCHI

2¼ pounds Kabocha Pumpkin (or any other type of dry firm-fleshed pumpkin)
¾ cup unbleached all purpose flour

¼ cup Parmigiano-Reggiano cheese, grated
⅛ teaspoon nutmeg, freshly grated
Salt to taste

SAUCE

2 shallots, minced
2 tablespoons unsalted butter
½ pound mascarpone cheese
½ cup Parmigiano-Reggiano cheese, grated

Salt and pepper to taste
1 tablespoon Italian parsley, finely chopped

Preheat oven to 400 degrees. Bake the pumpkin until tender when pierced with a knife. Pass through the fine disk of a potato ricer. Cool. Pour pumpkin onto a counter. Add flour, Parmigiano cheese, nutmeg and salt and work together into a dough. Cut into 4 pieces and roll each into finger-thick logs. Cut into ½-inch pieces and press each piece over the reversed tines of a fork. Place the gnocchi on a floured baking pan one by one as they are ready. Bring a large pot of salted water to a boil. Carefully drop in the gnocchi. As they rise to the surface, remove them with a large slotted spoon and into a bowl of ice water.

Meanwhile to make the sauce, sauté the shallots in the butter for 5 minutes. Fold in the mascarpone, Parmigiano, salt, pepper and cook over high heat for 1 minute. Then add the gnocchi, draining them carefully, to the pan and continue cooking for 1 minute until the gnocchi are coated with the sauce. Serve hot. Garnish with the fresh parsley.

Approximately 6 to 8 servings

SPINACH FETTUCCINE WITH PRAWNS

Chef Graziano Perozzi, Graziano's Ristorante

FRESH TOMATO SAUCE

4 large plump ripe tomatoes	1 tablespoon chopped shallots
4 tablespoons extra virgin olive oil	2 basil leaves
	1 cup water

Drop tomatoes in boiling water for 2 to 3 minutes. Remove and run under cold water to remove skin. Chop in blender. Heat oil in skillet with shallots and basil leaves. When shallots brown, add tomatoes and 1 cup of water. Boil for 15 to 30 minutes and simmer for another 30 minutes.

PASTA

1 pound green fettuccine	1 tablespoon chopped shallots
Oil	1 tablespoon chopped garlic
16 large prawns	2 cups fresh tomato sauce
Flour	1 cup white wine
Pinch of salt and pepper	

Precook pasta, set aside to cool. Heat oil in skillet. Flour prawns, add to skillet and sauté until cooked (white in color). Pour off oil. Add salt and pepper, shallots and garlic. Brown and then add wine to simmer for 2 minutes. Add tomato sauce, simmer for another 2 minutes. Add pasta and heat to taste.

4 servings

PENNE SEMOLINA

Chef Jose Perez, Semolina

½ pound penne pasta	4 ounces butter
1 tablespoon chopped garlic	8 ounces chicken breast
1 tablespoon chopped green onion	2 ounces white wine
1 ounce sun-dried tomatoes, chopped	1 handful of spinach
	Salt and pepper to taste

Cook pasta and drain when finished. Sauté butter with garlic, green onions and sun-dried tomatoes. Cook until butter is completely melted. Add chicken. Cook approximately 7 minutes. Add white wine. Cook for another 3 to 4 minutes. Add spinach and cooked pasta. Toss in sauté pan. Add salt and pepper to taste.

2 servings

LAMB SHANK RAVIOLI

Chef Jesse Mallgren, Madrona Manor

1 medium yellow onion, cut
  into ½-inch squares
2 cloves garlic
3 carrots, 2 peeled and cut
  into ½-inch pieces
4 stalks celery, 2 cut into ½-inch
  pieces
1 bottle (750 ml) red wine
2 cups veal stock
5 pounds lamb shank cut into
  2-inch pieces

1 bay leaf
5 whole black peppercorns
5 sprigs fresh thyme
2 tablespoons olive oil
1 ounce fresh truffle or
  2 tablespoons truffle oil
½ cup freshly grated Parmesan
  cheese
1 lemon, juiced
2 tablespoons salt

Caramelize onion, garlic, carrot and celery pieces in a heavy-bottomed pan. Add red wine and reduce by half. Add veal stock and bring to a boil. Add lamb shank and bay leaf, peppercorns and thyme. Cover pot with a piece of parchment paper, place in a preheated 325 degree oven and cook for 6 hours or until meat is tender and falling off the bone. Carefully remove pieces of lamb shank from the pan and let cool. Strain liquid through a fine strainer and put in the refrigerator. When stock has cooled completely remove any fat that may be on top of the liquid. Pick meat off bones. Be very careful when separating meat from the bones. You will need to pick through the meat several times to remove all small bone pieces and any gristle.

Rough chop the lamb shank meat and mix with chopped truffle and Parmesan cheese, season to taste. Make raviolis using fresh pasta.

Peel remaining celery stalk and cut into matchstick size pieces. Cook celery in 2 cups water with lemon juice and 2 tablespoons salt for ½ hour or until tender. Peel carrot and cut into very small dice. Sauté carrots and set aside. You will need about ½ cup of lamb shank braising liquid for 5 ravioli. Toss cooked ravioli and 5 pieces of braised celery in the lamb shank braising jus and simmer for 1 minute, season to taste. Place ravioli in a bowl and top with 1 tablespoon of the cooked carrots and cheese.

GNOCCHI GORGONZOLA E NOCI

Potato Dumplings in a Creamy Gorgonzola and Walnut Sauce

Chef Dennis, Cucina Paradiso Ristorante Italiano

GNOCCHI

2 pounds potatoes	Pinch of nutmeg
2 whole eggs	2 ounces Parmesan cheese
1½ pounds all purpose flour	Salt and pepper to taste

Preheat oven to 350 degrees. Wash the potatoes, then place them in oven and cook until soft, approximately 45 minutes. Cut the potatoes lengthwise and scoop them out. Beat the eggs and mix with the potatoes. Add the flour, nutmeg, Parmesan cheese, salt and pepper. Start kneading the mash on a working surface; take particular care to leave no lumps. Next take a piece of the dough, sprinkle with some flour and roll it into a sausage-like shape. Slice the cylinder of dough into little squares. Cook the gnocchi in abundant salted boiling water. They are ready when you see them float to the surface. Put the gnocchi in a separate pan and add the Gorgonzola and walnut cream sauce to taste. Cook for about 3 minutes. Serve while hot.

CREAM OF GORGONZOLA AND WALNUT SAUCE

1 tablespoon butter	1 ounce Parmesan cheese
2 cups heavy cream	¼ cup crushed walnuts
2 ounces Gorgonzola cheese	Salt and pepper to taste

Melt the butter in a saucepan. Add cream and cheeses. Stir until ingredients have become amalgamated. Add the walnuts, salt and pepper to taste.

4 to 6 servings

FAVA BEAN-SWEET POTATO RAVIOLIS IN MASAMAN CURRY SAUCE

Pacific Connection Catering for Rodney Strong Vineyards

Suggested wine: Reserve Chardonnay

PASTA DOUGH

1¾ cups all purpose flour
¼ cup semolina flour
1 teaspoon salt

6 egg yolks
2 whole eggs
2 teaspoons olive oil

Add dry ingredients in bowl. Mix the eggs with olive oil and slowly add to the dry ingredients. Mix on low speed for about 5 minutes. Remove dough and wrap in plastic and let it rest for 30 minutes.

FAVA BEAN AND SWEET POTATO FILLING

1 sweet potato
2 pounds fresh fava beans (you will need ½ cup shelled)

½ cup mascarpone cheese
Salt and pepper to taste

Bake the sweet potato in a 375 degree oven for about 45 minutes or until it is cooked. Remove the skin and mash in a bowl. Shell and peel the fava beans and cook in boiling salted water until they are soft, about 5 minutes. Mash with the sweet potato. Stir in mascarpone, salt and pepper. Set aside.

TO MAKE RAVIOLIS

Roll the pasta through a pasta machine, starting with it being thick and working it down until it is thin enough that you can see your fingers through the pasta. Mix 2 eggs with 2 tablespoons of water and brush on pasta. Put about ½ teaspoon of filling and cover with another sheet of pasta. Squeeze around the filling to let out the air and cut with an inch-round cutter. Place on a baking sheet with sprinkled semolina flour and set aside.

CURRY SAUCE

3 teaspoons masaman curry paste (found in Asian food sections)
3 cups chicken stock

1 cup heavy cream
½ cup crème fraîche
Salt and pepper to taste

Put all ingredients in a thick pot, reduce until about 1½ cups, blend in a blender and keep warm on the stove. Cook raviolis in boiling water and gently remove. Place with the sauce and gently coat.

8 servings

Windsor Vineyards

Windsor Vineyards is the oldest and largest direct-to-the consumer winery in America. Established in 1959, Windsor has produced award-winning wines in Sonoma County for more than 40 years, and is consistently in the ranks of the top three award winning U.S. wineries. Windsor held the number one ranking for 1998, 1999, and 2000.

Winemaker Toni Stockhausen has the resources and talent to make a variety of wine styles, and Windsor offers more than 40 different wines to suit a broad range of tastes and occasions. The wines are only available thorough Windsor's catalogues, telephone wine consultants and tasting rooms, and the wines can be delivered to customers in 26 states. The winery has tasting rooms in Healdsburg and Tiburon, California, and Marlboro, New York.

P.O. Box 368
Windsor, CA 95492
(800) 333-9987
www.windsorvineyards.com

Flamingo Resort Hotel and Conference Center

Sonoma County's fun, unique resort destination is located on 12 acres of beautifully landscaped grounds.

The 170-room Flamingo is ideally situated in central Sonoma County, a full-service Resort Hotel with 18,000 square feet of banquet facilities plus live weekend entertainment in the nightclub.

The Terrace Grill restaurant features fresh local Sonoma County cuisine. Also available, a world-class health club and spa.

2777 Fourth Street
Santa Rosa, CA 95405-4795
(707) 545-8530

Cline Cellars

Cline Cellars has garnered tremendous acclaim for intense, concentrated Zinfandels and unique Rhone-style wines. Our Ancient Vines Carignane, Zinfandel and Mourvedre wines are produced from some of the oldest and most rare vines in California.

Once the site of a Miwok Village and the first camp of the Sonoma Mission, this historic property has spectacular sweeping views of the Carneros valley. The tasting room is located inside an original 1850's farmhouse, and is enclosed by a large old-fashioned wrap-around porch for enjoyable outdoor seating. The grounds, with lush green lawns and sweeping willow trees, are surrounded by warm mineral springs. Springtime features the glorious, fragrant blossoms of more than 5,000 rose bushes.

The Cline family invites you to enjoy our wine tasting and picnic areas. Please contract us if we can be of any assistance in planning a personalized tour, catered luncheon, unique wine and food pairing, or any special moment of your life.

24737 Highway 121, Sonoma, CA 95475
(707) 940-4000

Big John's Market

Patterson '02

Big John's Market

This unique, newly remodeled and expanded deli and market in Healdsburg offers residents and travelers alike a broad range of deli and bakery items, fresh meats and produce, hand made sushi, Chester Fried Chicken and an extensive, comprehensive wine selection.

"Big John" is not a personal nickname for owner John Lloyd who, with wife Kim bought the business in 1994. Instead, BIG is an acronymn for Better Independent Grocers.

Big John's Market is proud to be the number one deli and market in Healdsburg whose motto is "Our Goal Is Your Satisfaction. You are invited to visit the website at

http/www.bigjohnsmarket.com
1345 Healdsburg Ave. at Dry Creek
Road, Healdsburg, CA
(707) 433-7161

Semolina

One of Petaluma's newest restaurants, Semolina offers Italian specialties that reflect the 50 years of experience of their chefs, Joe Peirano and John Perez, who say "in our menu you will find recipes and dishes we have collected throughout our careers, some from family, some from friends, some from coworkers, all from the heart."

Join them in bringing a taste of classic Italian food into your life.

Within weeks of opening, Semolina was receiving great reviews from food critics, quickly becoming one of Petaluma's more popular dining destinations.

600 East Washington Street
Petaluma, CA 94952
(707) 766-6975

Spring Hill Jersey Cheese Co.

is an open-to-the public, rural cheese company specializing in a wide range of specialty cheeses made from 100% rich Jersey milk. Tours are offered year-round to give consumers a chance to experience the fine art of hand-made, home-made cheese production.

Spring Hill cheese specialties include White Cheddar, Sage Cheddar, Quark (a spread), Horseradish Jack, Spring Hill Breeze, Fresh Curd, Diana, Teleme, Dry Jack and Mike Firehouse.

Spring Hill cheeses are available at area stores, local farmer's markets, and can be ordered online at springhillcheese.com.

For those seeking to tour Spring Hill Jersey Cheese Co., all that is required is calling (707) 762-3446 to arrange the tour. There are attractions for the kids as well as adults. In the fall, we feature a pumpkin patch and potato fields.

Spring Hill Jersey Cheese Co.
4235 Spring Hill Road
Petaluma, CA 94952
(707) 762-3446

Healdsburg Area

MORE SPECIALTIES

MAMA'S PAELLA

Carol Kozlowski-Every, Kozlowski Farms

1 pound fresh clams
1 pound fresh mussels
½ pound calamari (squid) cut in 1-inch pieces
½ pound medium shrimp, unpeeled
½ pound bay scallops
½ cup Spanish olive oil, divided
3 boneless chicken breasts, cut in half
3 boneless center cut pork chops, cut in half
2 Spanish style chorizo, cut in 1-inch diagonal pieces
1 large yellow onion, finely chopped
2 ripe tomatoes, peeled and chopped

1 teaspoon salt
¼ teaspoon freshly ground pepper
2 cups white rice
2 cups water
1 10½-ounce can chicken broth
1 cup dry white wine
1 small red bell pepper, chopped
8 ounces small frozen peas
8 ounces frozen artichoke hearts, cut each piece in half
3 medium garlic cloves, mashed in a mortar
1 teaspoon Spanish saffron
12 asparagus tips, steamed and cooled (optional for garnish)
1 jar pimento strips (optional for garnish)

Scrub clams and mussels. Wash remaining seafood and set aside.

In a heavy Dutch oven skillet, heat ¼ cup olive oil. Brown chicken pieces, set aside and keep warm. Brown pork pieces, set aside and keep warm. Brown chorizo, drain on paper towel, set aside and keep warm.

Wash skillet. Heat remaining ¼ cup olive oil. Cook onions until transparent. Add tomatoes, salt and pepper and cook for 5 minutes. Add rice, water, chicken broth and wine. Stir to combine. Add red bell peppers. Cover and cook for 20 minutes over medium heat. Add frozen peas, artichoke hearts, bay scallops, calamari, mashed garlic and saffron. Fold all ingredients together.

Have your oven preheated to 375 degrees. Place covered Dutch oven in preheated oven and continue to bake for 20 minutes.

To finish remaining seafood, place clams and mussels in a heavy pot with 1 cup of water. Bring to a boil for 2 minutes. Add shrimp and continue cooking until shells of clams and mussels open, about another 2 minutes.

In a large shallow paella dish, layer cooked rice ingredients, chicken, pork, chorizo and shrimp. Arrange opened clams, mussels, asparagus and pimentos on top. Place back in 375 degree oven for 10 minutes to make sure paella is heated through.

6 to 8 servings

SPIEDINI DI FONTINA

Fontina Kebabs

Chef Maria Belmonte, Caffé Portofino

10 ounces fontina cheese
¼ pound smoked pancetta
  bacon
8 slices bread
2 egg yolks
1 cup hot béchamel sauce

½ cup all purpose flour
1 egg, beaten
Salt and pepper to taste
¾ cup breadcrumbs
2 cups vegetable oil

Cut fontina and pancetta into 20 cubes each. Remove crust from bread and cut into quarter slices. On 4 skewers put 5 cubes of cheese alternating bread, fontina and pancetta. Add 2 egg yolks to hot béchamel with a pinch of pepper and dip skewers in to coat and allow to cool. First dip skewers in flour, then in beaten egg with a pinch of salt. Finally, cover kabobs in breadcrumbs. Fry in hot oil until golden brown. Continue process until all cubes are fried. Drain on paper towels, lay on dish and serve.

4 servings

WINE COUNTRY PAELLA

Won 2002 Sonoma County Harvest Fair Best of Show

Chef Robin Lehnhoff, Lake Sonoma Winery

3 cups basmati rice
3 tablespoons butter
2 teaspoons saffron threads, divided
1 pound rock shrimp
1 pound PEI mussels
Olive oil
2 tablespoons chopped garlic, divided
Splash of your favorite wine
1 cup diced onion
1 tablespoon chopped shallots
1 cup diced sweet red pepper
1 cup diced pasilla pepper
2 jalapeño peppers, seeded and minced
1 pound andouille sausage, sliced
1 pound chicken meat, cooked and diced
3 cups canned diced tomatoes in juice
½ cup chopped fresh parsley
½ cup chopped fresh oregano
Salt and pepper to taste

Cook rice in pot of boiling water with salt, 1 teaspoon saffron and butter. Cook until tender. Strain out water (like when cooking pasta). Pour saffron rice into a large bowl that can accommodate all the other ingredients. Set aside while preparing remaining ingredients.

In a sauté pan, sauté rock shrimp just until done and set aside. Cook mussels by sautéing in olive oil and garlic until the mussels are warm...then add a splash of your favorite wine and cover to finish cooking. Mussels are cooked when they pop open. Remove from heat immediately. Set seafood aside.

In sauté pan, sauté diced onion, shallots and garlic and sweat. Add peppers, sausage, chicken and canned tomatoes and juice. Let simmer for 10 minutes. Add 1 more teaspoon of saffron to this and let simmer for 15 more minutes to blend the flavors. Add fresh herbs, cooked seafood and season with salt and pepper.

Pour into saffron rice and combine. Paella is traditionally served in a large shallow cast iron skillet. A chafing dish can be used or a large platter is nice to show how grand this dish truly is.

LEMON GARLIC CHICKEN PITA

Chef Vicky M. Walker, Doubletree Hotel

1 large onion, julienned
1 red bell pepper, julienned
3 tablespoons minced garlic
¼ cup vegetable oil
4 6-ounce chicken thighs,
　julienned

1 tablespoon fresh oregano
3 tablespoons lemon juice
Salt and pepper to taste
4 pita breads
2 tomatoes diced
4 ounces shredded lettuce

Sauté onions, red bell pepper and garlic in oil. Add chicken, oregano, lemon and salt and pepper. Warm pitas and fill with chicken, tomato and lettuce. Top with 3 ounces Tzatziki (recipe on page 218).

4 servings

ASPARAGUS SOUFFLÉ

Chef Christian Bertrand, Glen Ellen Restaurant and Cottages

3 ounces unsalted butter
1½ ounces flour
½ pint milk
5 egg yolks
¾ ounce Gruyère, grated
3 ounces asparagus spears

Cayenne pepper
3 egg whites
½ pint beurre blanc
¼ ounce tomato purée
Salt and black pepper
4 pinches chervil

Make roux with butter and flour. Bring milk to boil and add to roux, stirring to make smooth. Beat the egg yolks and incorporate into mixture. Cook over low heat for 5 minutes. Add Gruyère. Steam asparagus until al dente. Cut tips to 1½ inches long. Dice stalks and add to sauce. Season with cayenne. Butter 3½-inch ramekins. Whisk egg whites until stiff and fold into warm asparagus sauce with spoon. Bake at 400 degrees for 25 minutes.

Warm beurre blanc and pour on each plate. Unmold soufflés and place on each plate. Garnish with tomato purée, chervil and asparagus tips.

4 servings

TZATZIKI

Chef Vicky M. Walker, Doubletree Hotel

½ cucumber, peeled, seeded
    and grated
1 cup yogurt
2 cloves garlic, minced
1 tablespoon dill, finely chopped

1 tablespoon olive oil
1 tablespoon lemon juice
1 cup sour cream
Salt to taste

Add grated cucumber to yogurt. Add remaining ingredients to yogurt mixture and mix well. Season with salt.

2 cups

BAKED POLENTA
WITH FONTINELLA CHEESE

Vella Cheese Company

Polenta is layered with Fontinella cheese and cream in this decadent casserole. Offer it with sausages and tomato sauce, or on its own as a brunch or lunch dish.

4¾ cups water, divided
2 14½-ounce cans chicken
    broth
5 shallots, minced
4 teaspoons dried marjoram

2½ cups yellow cornmeal
Salt and pepper
1 pound Vella Fontinella
    cheese, grated
½ cup whipping cream

Butter 8 x 13-inch baking dish. Combine 2¼ cups water, broth, shallots and marjoram in heavy large Dutch oven and bring to a boil. Mix 2½ cups cold water and cornmeal in bowl. Gradually mix cornmeal mixture into broth mixture. Return to boil, stirring constantly. Reduce heat to medium and boil gently until polenta is very thick, stirring often, about 10 minutes. Season with salt and pepper.

Immediately spread 2 cups polenta in prepared dish. Top with 1¾ cups cheese. Drizzle with ¼ cup cream. Repeat layering, using 2 cups polenta, 1¾ cups cheese and ¼ cup cream. Top with remaining polenta. Spread remaining cheese over. Cover with foil. (Can be made 1 day ahead. Cover and chill. Bring to room temperature before continuing.) Preheat oven to 350 degrees. Bake covered polenta until hot in center, about 1 hour, 15 minutes. Uncover, continue baking until polenta bubbles at edges and top begins to brown, about 10 minutes.

10 servings

PISELLI BRASSATI

Peas Braised with Lettuce

Chef Michael Ghilarducci, The Depot Hotel, Cucina Rustica

2 tablespoons sweet butter
1 medium onion, finely diced
1 pound fresh peas (or 1 pound
   frozen petits pois)

½ head iceberg lettuce, finely
   julienned
Salt and pepper to taste

Melt the butter in a heavy pan and sauté the onions over
medium heat until transparent. Add the peas to the onions. If
the peas are fresh, cook them for 4 to 5 minutes with the onion
before adding the lettuce. (If the peas are frozen, add the peas
and lettuce to the onions at the same time.) Once the lettuce is
added, simmer for 5 minutes, until the peas are tender and the
lettuce wilted. Remove the lid. If there seems to be excess
liquid, turn up the heat and reduce the liquid rapidly over high
heat. Salt and pepper to taste.

4 servings

GRILLED PORTOBELLA AND EGGPLANT SANDWICH WITH PESTO MAYONNAISE

Chef Vicky M. Walker, Doubletree Hotel

1 eggplant cut into 8 slices
4 medium portobella
   mushrooms, stemmed and
   cleaned
½ cup olive oil
Salt and pepper
4 focaccia buns

Pesto mayonnaise (see below)
2 roasted red bell peppers (jar
   or canned)
8 slices fresh mozzarella
4 romaine lettuce leaves
2 Roma tomatoes, sliced

Toss eggplant slices and mushrooms in olive oil and season with
salt and pepper. Grill eggplant and mushrooms until soft. Toast
buns. Spread pesto mayonnaise on buns. Layer ¼ of the eggplant, mushroom and roasted red bell pepper plus 2 slices of
mozzarella on bottom of each bun. Place under broiler until
cheese is melted. Garnish with lettuce and tomatoes.

PESTO MAYONNAISE
¾ cup mayonnaise

¼ cup prepared pesto

Mix.

4 servings

CATAPLANA A ALGARVIA

Mussels, Pork and Linguiça Stewed with Tomatoes, Bell Peppers, Onion and White Wine, Served with Chopped Cilantro

Chef Manuel Azevedo, LaSalette Restaurant

½ cup smoked bacon, diced
2 links linguiça, sliced ½-inch thick at a diagonal
1 tablespoon olive oil
½ pound lean pork, cubed
1 medium yellow onion, diced
2 red bell peppers, diced
¼ cup garlic cloves, sliced thin
3 cups tomato juice
Portuguese Spice Blend (recipe below)
1 teaspoon paprika

¼ teaspoon cumin powder
Pinch each of nutmeg, allspice, cloves and cinnamon
¼ teaspoon crushed red pepper
2 bay leaves
2 pounds mussels, scrubbed and bearded
3 medium tomatoes, diced
1 cup white wine
Salt and pepper to taste
Cilantro, chopped

PORTUGUESE SPICE BLEND *(great for other dishes and marinades)*
1 teaspoon paprika
¼ teaspoon cumin powder

Pinch each of nutmeg, allspice, cloves and cinnamon

In a large sauté pan, brown bacon and linguiça with olive oil over medium heat. Add pork and sauté until light brown. Add onion and bell peppers. Sauté for 5 minutes on low heat stirring often, being careful not to burn. Add garlic, tomato juice, Portuguese spice blend, crushed red pepper and bay leaves. Simmer for 20 minutes covered. Layer mussels on top of stewed mixture. Sprinkle diced tomato over mussels and add white wine. Bring mixture to a boil. When mussels are open, sprinkle with chopped cilantro and serve with crusty bread.

6 servings

ARTICHOKE AND PESTO AÏOLI

Chef Randy Hoppe, Catelli's The Rex

2 artichokes whole
Salt
1 tablespoon lemon juice

1 tablespoon olive oil
2 ounces white wine

Boil artichokes in hot water with salt and lemon juice until tender, 45+ minutes. Remove immediately and place in ice bath to cool. Cut cooled artichokes in half and place cut side down in oil in a sauté pan. Sauté over medium heat until a thin crust forms on the bottom, approximately 2 minutes. Splash with wine and cover pan with lid. Steam until interior of choke is hot, approximately 2 minutes.

Serve artichoke with pesto aïoli for dipping.

PESTO AÏOLI
3 egg yolks
2 teaspoons lemon juice
1 cup corn/vegetable oil

¼ cup pesto sauce
Salt

Place egg yolks and lemon juice in a blender and pulse until blended. Very slowly drizzle in oil in a thin, steady stream until thickened (2 to 3 minutes). Add pesto and pulse to blend. Add salt to taste. (For a quick version, mix pesto sauce and commercial mayonnaise.)

4 servings

DUNGENESS CRAB-PICKLED WATERMELON RIND-BASIL SALAD

with Watermelon Gazpacho

Executive Chef Randy Lewis, Kendall-Jackson Wine Estates, Ltd.

When I think of growing up in those hot muggy days of summer in the South, watermelon comes to mind. It offers such a cooling character to those humid days. New Orleans cuisine is diffidently French-influenced, but the Africans, Islanders and Spaniards also shaped this wonderful cuisine. This dish was inspired by that classic Spanish soup, Gazpacho, some Southern favorites and the beautiful Dungeness crab found on the Sonoma Coast.

WATERMELON GAZPACHO

½ seedless watermelon, flesh diced and reserve rind
½ red onion, diced
1 red bell pepper, seeded and diced
1 English cucumber, diced, peeled and seeded

1 jalapeño pepper, seeded and minced
3 garlic cloves, minced
1 celery stalk
2 tablespoons sherry vinegar
Salt, pepper, vinegar, lemon juice to taste

Place ingredients in blender and purée. Season with salt and pepper. Chill. Before serving readjust seasoning with salt, pepper, vinegar and lemon juice.

PICKLED WATERMELON RIND

3 cups water
1 cup sherry vinegar
1 cup white wine vinegar
2 cups brown sugar
24 black peppercorns
¼ cinnamon stick
1 bay leaf

1 jalapeño pepper
1 tablespoon coriander seeds
½ teaspoon fennel seeds
2 cloves
1 tablespoon kosher salt
1 cup watermelon rind, peeled and diced ¼-inch

Combine all ingredients except watermelon rind in a pot and simmer for 15 minutes and strain. Add liquid and rind to a pot and simmer until translucent but still al dente. Strain and cool rind.

DUNGENESS CRAB-PICKLED WATERMELON RIND-BASIL SALAD

1 pound Dungeness crabmeat	¼ cup basil chiffonade
½ cup pickled watermelon rind	2 tablespoons olive oil
	Salt and pepper

Combine all ingredients in a bowl and season with salt and pepper.

TO ASSEMBLE

Place salad in center of cold soup bowl and drizzle Gazpacho around and serve.

4 servings

SUMMER CHANTERELLE, CIPOLLINI ONION AND TALEGGIO CHEESE OMELET

Chef Eve Litke, The Farm House

2 cipollini onions, chopped	3 farm fresh eggs
1 ounce unsalted butter, divided	1 tablespoon heavy cream
Pinch of fresh thyme	2 ounces Taleggio cheese
4 ounces summer chanterelle mushrooms, sliced	Salt and pepper

Sauté the onions in half the butter until softened. Add chopped thyme and mushrooms. Cook until almost dry and set aside. Beat eggs in bowl and add cream. In a nonstick pan, melt remaining butter, add eggs and cook for 1 minute at low heat. Add onions, mushrooms and cheese. Fold over each side and serve on warmed plate with truffle potato cake.

TRUFFLE POTATO CAKE

1 clove garlic, sliced	1 large Yukon gold potato, thinly grated on a mandolin
1 ounce olive oil	
12 ounces stemmed spinach	1 ounce peanut oil
	Drizzle of white truffle oil

Sauté the garlic in olive oil until lightly browned. Add spinach, cook until wilted. Let cool, squeeze, dry and chop small. Squeeze potato dry, place half in a hot pan with peanut oil, top with spinach and top with remaining potato. Salt and pepper to taste. Cook until brown on both sides and cut into wedges. Drizzle with truffle oil.

2 servings

PARMESAN FLAN

with Spring Asparagus and Truffle Butter Sauce

Chef Eve Litke, The Farm House

FLAN

1 tablespoon unsalted butter	2 egg yolks
2 tablespoons all purpose flour	1 cup grated Parmesan cheese
1½ cups half-and-half	¼-½ teaspoon salt
½ cup heavy cream	Pinch of white pepper
1 whole egg	Dash of nutmeg

Butter 8 2-ounce ramekins. Melt butter in small heavy saucepan. Add flour and cook until aroma turns nutty. Slowly whisk in the half-and-half and cream. Cook for 3 to 4 minutes. Remove from heat. Add egg and egg yolks one at a time, whisking well after each addition. Add the Parmesan, salt, pepper and nutmeg. Strain through fine strainer. Ladle mixture into ramekins. Place ramekins in large baking pan. Pour enough water to come up half-way. Place in 350 degree oven for 20 minutes.

ASPARAGUS WITH TRUFFLE BUTTER SAUCE

32 spears spring asparagus, blanched for 2 minutes, placed in ice bath and drained	3 ounces truffle butter or 3 ounces unsalted butter with 1 tablespoon truffle oil
1 cup chicken or vegetable stock	Salt and pepper to taste Chopped parsley

Bring stock to a boil, add asparagus to heat through. Add butter and reduce to sauce consistency. Season with salt and pepper, parsley and truffle oil if using.

TO SERVE

Unmold warm flan onto plate. Arrange spears of asparagus around flan. Spoon butter sauce over asparagus. Garnish with watercress or fava bean shoots if you like.

8 servings

ONE PAN MEAL

Chef Angelo Ibleto, Angelo's Italian Taste

1 onion, chopped
2 links fresh Italian turkey
   sausages
¼ cup white wine

4 cooked red potatoes (leave
   skin on), cubed
3 tablespoons Angelo's Italian
   Mustard or Garlic Mustard

Sauté onions in olive oil until golden brown. Add sausage and
wine, cook until meat has cooked through. Add potatoes and
Angelo's Italian Mustard and stir to blend all ingredients.
Continue to cook until potatoes begin to brown. Serve with
salad and Italian bread.

2 servings

CORN CAKES

Chef Robert Buchshachermaier, Café Europe

¾ cup all purpose flour
½ cup polenta
1 teaspoon salt
1 teaspoon sugar
½ teaspoon baking powder
½ teaspoon baking soda
1¼ cups buttermilk

2 tablespoons butter, melted
1 large egg
1 cup corn kernels, if using
   frozen—thawed
½ cup chopped green onions
Vegetable oil for frying

Mix first 6 ingredients in a bowl. Whisk buttermilk, melted
butter and egg. Gradually add dry ingredients. Purée ½ cup corn
and add to batter along with remaining corn and green onions.
Heat vegetable oil in large nonstick pan. Spoon batter into pan
by 2 spoonfuls, forming 3-inch cakes. Cook until golden.

LEEK AND MUSTARD GALETTE

Michele Anna Jordan

Be sure to clean leeks thoroughly, as dirt and sand tends to hide in the leaves. The St. George cheese is, of course, from our very own Joe Matos Cheese Factory, one of Sonoma County's most charming treasures.

CRUST
1 cup all purpose flour
¾ teaspoon kosher salt
1 teaspoon whole black
   peppercorns, ground

6 tablespoons butter, chilled
   and cut into cubes
¼ cup ice water

FILLING
6 medium leeks, white and
   pale green parts only,
   trimmed and thoroughly
   rinsed and dried
3 tablespoons butter
⅓ cup water
Kosher salt
Black pepper in a mill
2 tablespoons Dijon-type
   mustard, divided

6 ounces St. George cheese,
   grated
1 tablespoon minced fresh
   chives
1 egg white, mixed with
   1 tablespoon water
1 teaspoon coarse sea salt or
   Hawaiian alaea salt

First, make the galette dough. Combine flour, salt and ground black pepper in a small bowl and use your fingers or pastry cutter to work in the butter so that the mixture resembles coarse-ground cornmeal. Add the ice water, gently press the dough together, gather it up into a ball and wrap in plastic or wax paper. Chill for 1 hour.

Meanwhile, cut the leeks into thin (⅛-inch) rounds. Melt the butter in a heavy skillet set over medium heat, add the leeks and sauté for 5 minutes, tossing now and then as they cook. Add the water, stir and cook until the leeks are completely wilted. Season with salt and pepper, reduce the heat to medium-low and continue to cook until the leeks are very tender. Remove from the heat and stir in 1 tablespoon of the mustard. Set aside.

Preheat the oven to 400 degrees. Line a baking sheet with parchment paper and set it aside. Set the chilled dough on a floured work surface and use the palm of your hand to pat it flat. Roll it into a 14-inch circle about ⅛-inch thick and carefully transfer it to the parchment-lined baking sheet.

Brush the remaining mustard over the surface of the tart. Spread the cheese on top, leaving a 2-inch margin around the edges. Spread the leeks over the cheese, sprinkle the remaining cheese on top and scatter the chives over the cheese.

Gently fold the edges of the tart up and over the leeks and cheese, pleating the edges as you fold them. Using a pastry brush, brush the edge of the tart lightly with the egg wash and sprinkle it with the coarse salt or Hawaiian salt. Bake until the pastry is golden brown, about 35 to 40 minutes. Transfer to a rack to cool, cut into wedges and serve warm.

4 servings

OVERNIGHT APPLE FRENCH TOAST

Andy's Produce Market, Kathrin Skikos

2 large tart (Granny Smith) apples, peeled and sliced	3 eggs
½ cup butter	1 cup milk
1 cup packed brown sugar	1 teaspoon vanilla
2 tablespoons corn syrup	9 thick slices French bread

Place sliced apples in bottom of ungreased 9 x 13-inch pan. In a small saucepan, cook butter, brown sugar and syrup until thick (about 5 to 7 minutes). Pour over apples. Beat eggs with milk and vanilla, dip bread in egg mixture and place over apples. Cover and refrigerate overnight. Remove from refrigerator 30 minutes before baking. Bake uncovered for 35 minutes at 350 degrees.

4 servings

MAYAN CHILE RELLENOS

Chef Manuel Arjona, Maya Restaurant

4 large smooth-skinned
   poblano peppers, roasted
   and peeled
1½ cups finely diced spit-
   roasted chicken

1 cup roasted corn
1 cup finely chopped scallions
½ cup golden raisins
1½ cups breadcrumbs
4 tablespoons corn oil

Preheat oven to 350 degrees. Spray a large baking sheet with nonstick cooking spray. Carefully slit poblano peppers lengthwise. Remove and discard seeds and membranes. In a small bowl, combine remaining ingredients and shape into 4 bullet-shaped logs. Insert 1 log of stuffing into each prepared pepper, folding the sides of the peppers over the filling to enclose. Place stuffed peppers, seam side down, in a single layer on the prepared baking sheet. Brush evenly with oil. Bake 7 to 10 minutes, until peppers start to brown.

Serve with a sauce or salsa of your choice. The chile rellenos at Maya are served on an Orange-Tomato Cumin Sauce (recipe follows).

4 servings

ORANGE AND TOMATO SAUCE

Chef Manuel Arjona, Maya Restaurant

6 tablespoons cornstarch
2 tablespoons butter
4 tablespoons olive oil
2 onions, sliced
4 garlic cloves, chopped
½ tablespoon ground cumin

2½ tomatoes skinned, seeded
   and chopped, or 2 cans
   chopped tomatoes
1 cup fresh orange juice
Salt and pepper to taste

Heat cornstarch, butter and olive oil in a saucepan. Add the onions and garlic and cook for 5 minutes until softened but not colored. Stir in the ground cumin, tomatoes and orange juice. Bring to a boil, stir frequently for about 10 minutes until thickened. Add salt and pepper to taste.

CORN BOATS WITH
ZUCCHINI AND PEPPER JACK CHEESE

Vella Cheese Company

4 ears corn, unhusked
2 tablespoons olive oil
1 medium zucchini, cut into
⅓-inch dice
Salt

1 cup finely chopped red
onion
1 cup coarsely grated Vella
Jalapeño Monterey Jack
2 tablespoons finely crushed
corn tortilla chips

Pull a lengthwise strip of corn husk (about 1 to 1½ inches wide) from each ear to expose a strip of kernels and discard husk strip. Carefully peel back remaining husks, keeping them attached to stem ends, and snap ears from stem ends. Discard silk from husks. Tear a thin strip from a tender, inner piece of each husk to use it to tie loose end of each husk together forming a boat. Cut corn kernels from ears and discard cobs.

In a large heavy skillet heat oil over moderately high heat until hot but not smoking and sauté zucchini, stirring occasionally, until browned lightly and just tender, 2 to 3 minutes. Transfer zucchini with slotted spoon to a bowl and season with salt. In oil remaining in skillet, sauté corn kernels and onion with salt to taste over moderately high heat, stirring for 4 minutes. Then cook, covered, over low heat until corn is crisp-tender, 2 to 3 minutes. Add corn mixture to zucchini and season with salt.

Cool filling and stir in cheese. Spoon filling into husk boats. (Corn boats may be prepared up to this point 1 day ahead and kept chilled, covered.)

Preheat oven to 375 degrees. Arrange boats on a baking sheet and sprinkle filling with tortilla crumbs. Bake boats in upper third of oven until cheese is melted and filling is heated through, 15 to 20 minutes. Serve corn boats warm or at room temperature.

4 servings

RATATOUILLE STUFFED TOMATO

Chef Christine Topolos, Russian River Vineyards

Christine Topolos brought this inspiration of a dinner vegetable to us at Russian River Vineyards. It is tasty, attractive, and avoids the common restaurant blight of overcooked vegetables. In large kitchens with extensive staffs, this problem can be overcome by sautéing vegetables to order, but in the small kitchen at Russian River Vineyards that is not practical. This stuffed tomato allows us to give full attention to entrée preparation with assurance that the vegetable is always just right. This virtue may recommend it to you also. Prepare the tomatoes ahead of time, bake them, reduce the oven to low and turn your attention to last minute items.

8-10 tomatoes	1 large zucchini, 2 cups chopped
2 tablespoons olive oil	½ small eggplant, ¾ cup chopped
½ cup chopped onion	2 tablespoons minced fresh basil
1 tablespoon minced garlic	¼ teaspoon salt
1 large crookneck squash,	⅛ teaspoon black pepper
1½ cups chopped	1 cup chopped tomato meat

Begin by preparing the tomatoes. Cut off the top of each tomato at the stem end. Scoop out the insides with a grapefruit spoon or other implement. At Russian River Vineyards we use a butter curler, available at most kitchen shops. Use your hands to squeeze the juice and most of the seed from the tomatoes' insides and chop enough to make the 1 cup needed at the end of the recipe.

Heat olive oil in a skillet and add onion and garlic. Sauté a few minutes, stirring occasionally, then add the squashes and eggplant. Continue cooking 3 to 5 minutes, then add basil, seasonings and tomato meat. A minute or 2 more cooking will be sufficient. Cool the mixture, stuff it into the hollowed tomatoes, and top with breadcrumbs.

BREADCRUMBS

4 slices fresh sourdough bread	1½ tablespoons melted butter
3 tablespoons kasseri or	2 tablespoons chopped parsley
Parmesan cheese	Salt and pepper to taste

Remove crusts from bread, cut or tear into pieces. Process in blender or food processor until uniform; add cheese, melted butter and parsley. Season to taste. Store in a tightly covered container in the refrigerator.

8 to 10 servings

SMOKED SALMON WITH CAVIAR CRÈME FRAÎCHE, RED ONION AND CAPERS ON BOBOLI

Norma Poole and Joe Gentry, Cline Cellars

1 large Boboli (or other
    pre-made pizza crust)
8 ounces crème fraîche (or
    lightly whipped sour cream)

2 ounces caviar
8 ounces smoked salmon
½ cup chopped red onion
¼ cup capers

Preheat oven to 350 degrees. Heat Boboli for approximately 15 minutes. Take out of oven and spread evenly with crème fraîche mixed with caviar. Place slices of smoked salmon over entire crust, then layer with red onion and capers.

6 to 8 servings

QUINOA À LA PERUANA

Patty Karlin, Bodega Goat Cheese

2 large Bermuda onions
4 cloves garlic
1 red bell pepper, chopped
2 hot chili peppers, chopped
½-1 pound chicken cubed
    (optional)
2 medium-sized raw potatoes
2 cups quinoa

Salt and pepper to taste
¾ cup roasted salted peanuts
    (crushed with mortar and
    pestle)
½ pound (8-ounces) Queso
    Fresco cubed, just out of
    refrigerator

Chop onions and garlic very fine. Sauté with chopped peppers. Add chicken (optional). Chop potatoes in ¼-inch squares and sauté. Add rinsed quinoa. Continue to sauté for 5 minutes, stirring constantly over high flame. Cover with water ¾-inch above quinoa. Add salt and pepper. Simmer 30 to 40 minutes covered on low flame. Add peanuts and stir. Remove from stove. Stir in cubed Queso Fresco. Serve with white rice.

6 servings

MUSHROOM MEDLEY SAUTÉ WITH SOFT POLENTA

Chef Bob Engel, Gourmet Mushrooms, Inc.

5 cups water
1½ teaspoons salt
1 cup polenta
2 tablespoons olive oil
1 shallot, minced
1 clove garlic, minced

8 ounces sliced mixed
    mushrooms, such as Trumpet
    Royale™, Forest Nameko™,
    oyster mushrooms, or wilds
¼ cup Chardonnay
Fresh chopped parsley, thyme
    and/or rosemary
Salt and pepper to taste
½ cup grated Parmesan cheese

Bring water to the boil with salt. Add polenta in a steady stream while stirring briskly. Keep polenta at the bare simmer and stir frequently while preparing mushrooms.

Heat olive oil in a broad skillet. Add shallot and garlic. Cook a minute or so, then add the mushrooms. Toss or stir over medium heat for 5 minutes, add Chardonnay and continue cooking until wine is almost completely reduced. Remove from heat, add herbs and season to taste with salt and fresh ground pepper.

The polenta should be thick and creamy looking. The color will have changed from a bright yellow to a pastel yellow as the polenta lets go its starch. Stir most of the Parmesan into the polenta reserving a little for garnish. Portion polenta into bowls, top with sautéed mushrooms, garnish with additional grated Parmesan and herbs.

4 servings

OH! TOMMY BOY'S ROASTED FINGERLINGS

Oh! Tommy Boy's Organic Farm

3 cloves garlic, sliced
1 pound small fingerling
    potatoes, rinsed

1 pinch of rosemary
2 teaspoons olive oil

Sauté garlic, potatoes and rosemary in olive oil in a cast iron skillet for 5 minutes. Put in oven for 15 minutes at 350 degrees or until fork tender. Serve hot.

GRANDMA'S BAKED BEANS

Chef Lee Lombardi, Lombardi's Gourmet Deli

2 1-pound cans Pork 'n Beans
2 1-pound cans baked beans
1 pound bacon raw, 1-inch
   slices
1 cup ketchup
1 medium onion cut into ⅛-inch
   rounds
¼ teaspoon garlic powder
⅛ teaspoon each salt and
   pepper
¼ teaspoon liquid smoke
1 cup light brown sugar

Drain beans. Mix with other ingredients in a greased 9 x 12-inch glass baking dish. Cook at 250 degrees for 2 hours, stirring mixture occasionally until liquid is absorbed. Let cool 20 minutes before serving.

6 to 8 servings

RATATOUILLE

Chef Patrick Martin, Charcuterie

¼ cup olive oil
2 medium yellow onions,
   chopped
3 large green, red or yellow
   bell peppers, seeded,
   deribbed, cut into 1-inch
   cubes
1 head garlic, peeled and
   chopped
2 medium eggplants, peeled,
   cut into 1-inch cubes
4 medium zucchini, cut into
   1-inch cubes
2 tablespoons fresh thyme
1 bay leaf
3½-4 pounds tomatoes
   (10 to 12 medium-sized)
   peeled and chopped
¼ cup minced fresh basil

In a large saucepan, warm the olive oil. Add onions and sauté at low heat for about ½ hour or until onions are nice and golden. Add peppers and garlic. Sauté for 5 minutes. Add the rest of the ingredients and cook at low heat uncovered for 1½ to 2 hours.

4 to 6 servings

SPINACH MUSHROOM QUICHE

Spectrum Naturals/Spectrum Essentials

1 10-inch pie crust, baked

QUICHE LIQUID

3 eggs
1 cup milk
½ cup heavy cream

⅛ teaspoon nutmeg
Salt and pepper to taste

Using a whisk, beat the eggs in a large bowl, until light and well-blended. Add the milk, heavy cream, nutmeg, salt and pepper to taste. Whisk well to combine. You can prepare this quiche liquid a day in advance and refrigerate.

SPINACH MUSHROOM FILLING
May be prepared in advance and refrigerated for up to 2 days.

2 teaspoons Spectrum Naturals Organic Extra Virgin Olive Oil
10 cremini, button or shiitake mushrooms, sliced
1 clove garlic, finely chopped
1 clove shallot, finely chopped

1 10-ounce bag spinach, rinsed and drained in a colander and coarsely chopped
Salt and pepper to taste
1½ cups grated Swiss, mozzarella, Monterey Jack, fontina, manchego, or your favorite cheese, about 6 ounces

Preheat oven to 350 degrees. Heat the olive oil in a large skillet over medium heat. Add the mushrooms, garlic, shallot and spinach. Sprinkle evenly with salt and pepper. Cover and cook for about 2 minutes. Then using tongs, toss the spinach to coat with oil. Continue cooking, uncovered, for about 2 minutes, stirring occasionally, until the spinach is just wilted. Drain the spinach in a colander set into a bowl. Press out excess liquid using the back of a large spoon. Save the juices for a soup or sauce. Taste the spinach for seasonings.

Spray a cookie sheet with Spectrum Naturals Super Canola Skillet Spray or line it with parchment paper to catch any drips. Set the pre-baked pie crust onto the prepared cookie sheet. Sprinkle 1 cup of the cheese evenly on the crust. Arrange the spinach-mushroom mixture evenly in the crust. Then sprinkle the remaining cheese evenly over the top. Slowly pour the quiche liquid over the vegetables. Bake the quiche in the preheated oven for 1 hour, until the top is golden brown and the center is just set. The quiche will be puffy when you first remove it from the oven, then it will flatten within 10 minutes or so— so don't get alarmed when it does. Let set for 15 minute before cutting. Serve hot or at room temperature. Refrigerate any leftovers.

6 luncheon or light supper portions

Russian Gulch

Rodney Strong Vineyards
Sonoma County, California

Rodney D. Strong, one of the pioneers of the California wine industry, first came to California in 1959, seeking a place in California to start a winery.

In 1961, long before Sonoma County was "discovered" as a premium grape-growing region, Rod purchased 160 acres of vineyards in the county and the business was moved to the young wine region. Wine was made in an old winery building originally licensed in 1898. Then, in 1970, a new winery began construction just south of the sleepy hamlet of Healdsburg, where Rodney Strong Vineyards stands today.

In 1989, the Klein family, a hundred-year California farming family, purchased the winery and vineyards. CEO Tom Klein took ownership of some of the best vineyards in the county, one of which was the legendary "Alexander's Crown" vineyard in Alexander Valley.

The "Alexander's Crown," high atop a red volcanic slope overlooking the Russian River, was developed in 1971 and the 2001 vintage marked the 30th vintage of premium Cabernet Sauvignon produced from the vineyard. The "Alexander's Crown" Cabernet Sauvignon was the first vineyard designated red wine in Sonoma County.

Other of the fine vineyards owned by the winery are the "Charlotte's Home Vineyard" on the Alexander Valley floor along the Russian River. Downstream on the Russian River lie the winery's "River East" and "Jane's" vineyards.

In recent years, in an effort to become one of the most significant super premium wineries in Sonoma County, Tom Klein has purchased additional vineyards in the Russian River Valley and a breathtaking mountain vineyard at the very northern end of the Alexander Valley.

Considered by many as one of the county's greatest success stories, Rodney Strong Vineyards has thrived under the ownership of the Klein family.

The winery welcomes visitors seven days a week from 10 a.m. to 5 p.m. Come experience our Wine Gallery Tour.

11455 Old Redwood Highway

Healdsburg, CA 98448

(707) 431-1533

The Sonoma Cheese Factory
"Home of Sonoma Jack"

The famed Sonoma Jack Brand is a moist, semi-soft, rindless cheese, produced by the family at the plant and store located in Sonoma's historic Plaza. It was founded in 1931 by Celso Viviani, who traced his roots to the 11th century in Lucca, Italy. After arriving in the U.S., Celso worked for a local winery until Prohibition, when he began work producing cheese at the Sonoma Mission Creamery. Today, the business is run by his son Peter and grandson David.

Jack cheese, created by David Jacks in 1882 in Monterey, is California's first indigenous cheese, Teleme being the second. The Vivianis produce many different flavors of Sonoma Jack, from garlic to habanero, the hottest of the pepper cheeses. They also produce ricotta, Teleme, and Sonoma Cheddar.

You are invited to visit the Sonoma Cheese Factory to sample premium, award-winning Real California Cheeses, explore the wine department and the sumptuous gourmet food section and enjoy the outdoor patio grill.

As David Viviani says, "if the grape's leap to immortality is wine, then , milk's leap to immortality has to be cheese." The Sonoma Cheese Factory welcomes you to experience the unique and immortal gastronomic pleasures of Sonoma Valley.

2 Spain Street, "On the Plaza"

Sonoma, CA 95476

707-996-1931 or 1-800-367-1947

FAX 707-935-3535

237

Coleman Valley Road

DESSERTS

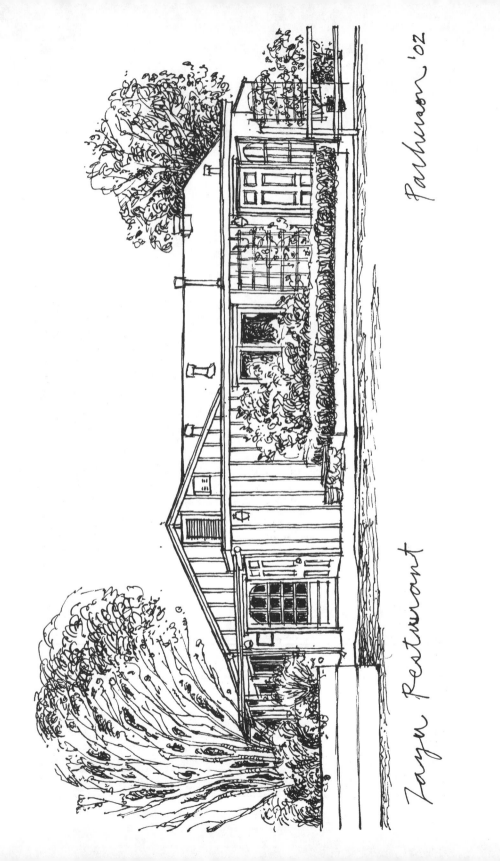

Zayo Restaurant

Parkinson '02

THE ZAZU BRÛLÉED BANANA SPLIT

Chef John Stewart, Zazu

This is a twist on the American classic and a tribute to Barbara Tropp who passed away this year. She served ginger ice cream with dark chocolate sauce that I still remember at China Moon in San Francisco a decade ago.

GINGER ICE CREAM

8 egg yolks
1 cup plus 2 tablespoons sugar
¼ teaspoon kosher salt
2¼ cups milk

2¼ cups cream
3 ounces fresh ginger, peeled
and grated

In a medium bowl, whisk the yolks, sugar and salt together. In a medium saucepan in medium high heat, scald the milk, cream and ginger. Remove from the heat and let steep 15 minutes. Set up an ice bath. Return the pan to medium high heat and bring the cream back up to a simmer. Slowly whisk into the yolks. Return the base to the saucepan on medium heat and stir constantly until the mixture coats the back of a wooden spoon, about 5 minutes. Cool in an ice bath and then refrigerate. Once completely cooled, strain ice cream base and freeze according to your ice cream maker's directions.

DARK CHOCOLATE SAUCE

3 tablespoons unsalted butter
8 ounces semi-sweet chocolate
¾ cup sugar
1 cup boiling water

¼ cup plus 2 tablespoons light
corn syrup
2 teaspoons vanilla extract

In a small saucepan on medium low heat, melt the butter, chocolate and sugar. Whisk in the boiling water and corn syrup. Bring to simmer about 5 minutes. Remove the chocolate sauce from the heat and add vanilla.

BANANA SPLIT

Half a banana per person
Sugar
Ginger ice cream

Dark chocolate sauce
(use your favorite or
follow our recipe)

Split the banana lengthwise and place on a cookie sheet. Sprinkle with sugar and use a torch to caramelize carefully (not to burn yourself). In an appropriate dish, place the brûléed banana, a few scoops of ginger ice cream and ladle over with warmed chocolate sauce.

BREAD PUDDING

Chef Joseph, Joseph's Restaurant and Bar

1 loaf French bread	½ tablespoon vanilla
6 eggs	½ cup sugar
6 cups milk	3 tablespoons honey
1 cup walnuts	1 cup raisins
1 cup almonds	

Cut bread in 1-inch squares. Mix remaining ingredients well and pour over bread. Bake at 425 degrees for approximately 45 minutes.

10 servings

STRAWBERRY AND TARRAGON SOUP WITH IRON HORSE ROSÉ GRANITÉ

Chef Mark Purdy, Dry Creek Kitchen

SOUP

3 cups strawberries, stems removed	⅓ cup sugar
⅓ cup Iron Horse Rosé	½ cup fresh orange juice
2 stems chopped tarragon	Juice of 1 lemon

Purée in a blender until smooth the berries, wine, half of the tarragon, half of the sugar, and half of the orange juice. Chill the purée and then adjust the consistency and flavor with the left over juices and sugar. Keep in refrigerator until service.

GRANITÉ

3 cups Iron Horse Rosé	Juice of 1 lemon
6 tablespoons sugar	⅓ cup honey

Combine all of the ingredients and pour into a freezer-safe shallow vessel. Freeze until the granité is opaque.

TO SERVE

Pour the chilled soup into 6 chilled bowls. Shave the granité by running a spoon along the surface of the ice. Gently pull a spoonful of ice from the pan and float it over the soup. Garnish with fresh tarragon leaves. Serve immediately.

6 servings

YOGURT CREAM

Chef Robert Buchshachermaier, Café Europe

I love this one in chocolate cups topped with berries. You can also use it as a filling in tartlets.

6 gelatin leaves
2 cups heavy cream
8½ ounces yogurt

3½ ounces powdered sugar
2 tablespoons lemon juice

Place gelatin leaves in cold water until soft. Whip cream until stiff. Mix yogurt, sugar and lemon juice. Put soft gelatin in a cup, place in hot water and let it melt. Add liquid gelatin into yogurt drop by drop. Fold in whipped cream. Refrigerate for a minimum of 2 hours.

6 servings

LAVENDER AND WILD FLOWER HONEY CRÈME BRÛLÉE

Chef Sondra Bernstein, the girl and the fig

1½ cups heavy cream
½ cup milk
3-4 sprigs lavender or
    1 tablespoon dried lavender
7 egg yolks

2 ounces sugar
2 ounces wild flower honey
3-4 tablespoons granulated
    sugar

Preheat oven to 350 degrees. Put cream and milk into a sauce-pan with lavender. Bring to a boil and turn off. Let stems steep for about 15 minutes or until the milk has a lavender flavor.

Meanwhile, beat the egg yolks, sugar and honey until smooth. Pull sprigs out of the cream and milk mixture and whisk into eggs. Strain through a fine mesh sieve and skim off any foam. Pour into 4-ounce ramekins or brûlée dishes. Set into a baking pan, add enough hot water to reach halfway up the sides. Place in oven and bake 25 to 30 minutes or until they are set. Test by jiggling the dish. Cool in the water bath. Refrigerate for a few hours or overnight.

Before serving, sprinkle tops with a thin layer of granulated sugar and caramelize with a small torch or under a high temperature broiler. Garnish with lavender blossoms or candied violets.

4 servings

RASPBERRY CHOCOLATE TRUFFLES

Carol Kozlowski-Every, Kozlowski Farms

Kimberly Every-Knechtle, daughter of Carol Kozlowski-Every, created this incredible (award winning!) truffle recipe when she was just 11 years old! Since then she has been profiled in several gourmet magazines, and has appeared on television demonstrating the simple how-to's of her Raspberry Chocolate Truffles.

1 pound bittersweet chocolate, broken into pieces
½ cup (4 ounces) raspberry liquor
10 egg yolks
1 cup butter cut into chunks, at room temperature
3 cups powdered sugar, sifted
¼ cup unsweetened cocoa powder
60 raspberries (optional)

Melt chocolate with raspberry liquor in a double boiler over medium heat. Remove and carefully whisk in egg yolks, one at a time. Add the butter a bit at a time, stirring well after each addition. Add ¼ of the powdered sugar at a time, beating after each addition. When all of the sugar has been incorporated, and the mixture is smooth, refrigerate, covered, until it is chilled through.

To roll truffles, take about 1½ teaspoons of mixture and roll in both hands (coat with a little cocoa powder first) until it forms a ball. Drop truffle in bowl with cocoa powder and agitate bowl so the truffle becomes fully coated with cocoa. Remove and set on a tray. Make a slight indentation in the top of the truffle and lightly press a raspberry into it so the berry stays in place. When all the truffles have been rolled, refrigerate until ready to serve. With fresh raspberries, serve within a day. Without raspberries and refrigerated in tightly sealed container, they will keep for a week or more.

60 truffles

DOUBLE APPLE TURNOVERS

Lee and Shirley Walker, Walker Apples

CRUST
3 cups flour
2 tablespoons sugar

2 sticks margarine
1 cup sour cream

Combine flour and sugar. Cut in margarine until crumbly. Mix in sour cream to form dough.

FILLING
3 cups chopped apples
¼ cup brown sugar
¾ cup applesauce

½ teaspoon cinnamon
¼ teaspoon mace

Combine apple, sugar, applesauce and spices. Roll dough into 6-inch squares. Put apple mixture on one corner, moisten edge of pastry and fold over. Place the turnovers on a large cookie sheet with a slight edge that has been sprayed with Pam. Brush turnovers with milk. Bake in a 350 degree oven for 20 to 30 minutes or until lightly browned. Remove immediately and cool on wire racks.

SPICED RASPBERRY SORBET

Chef Phil McGauley, Korbel Champagne Cellars

⅔ cup sugar
¼ cup water
1 tablespoon orange juice
⅓ cup brandy
1 tablespoon whole black
  peppercorns

1 teaspoon vanilla
1 cinnamon stick
2 cups raspberry purée
1 tablespoon balsamic vinegar

In a saucepan combine sugar, water, orange juice and brandy. Bring to a boil, stirring until sugar is dissolved. Stir in peppercorns, vanilla and cinnamon stick. Remove from heat, cover pan and let syrup sit for 1 hour. Strain syrup through a fine sieve into a food processor, add raspberry purée and vinegar. Purée until smooth. Strain one more time to remove any other solids. Freeze in ice cream maker. Serve with almond biscotti.

DEATH BY CHOCOLATE

Chef Phil McGauley, Kenwood Vineyards

15 ounces semi-sweet
  chocolate
1 cup heavy cream
2 ounces butter
4 egg yolks

¾ cup powdered sugar
¼ cup Kenwood Sonoma
  County Cabernet
  Sauvignon

Melt chocolate, butter and heavy cream in a bowl over simmering water. Remove from heat. Whisk the eggs into chocolate mixture one at a time. Whisk in sugar, then Cabernet. Line a loaf pan with plastic wrap and pour chocolate mixture into the pan. Let chocolate cool to room temperature. Cover and refrigerate overnight. Remove from loaf pan, remove plastic wrap and slice into ¼-inch thick slices. Serve with fruit sauce. IT'S TO DIE FOR!

BLACKBERRY SAUCE
1 bag frozen blackberries

Thaw the bag of blackberries. Purée, then strain. Drizzle onto the side of the plate for desired look.

15 servings

CABERNET TRUFFLES

Chef Laurie Souza, Korbel Champagne Cellars

6 tablespoons unsalted butter
2 tablespoons heavy cream

8 ounces bittersweet
  chocolate, chopped
¼ cup Cabernet Sauvignon

Bring the butter and cream to a simmer in a small saucepan. Remove pan from the heat and add the chocolate. Stir until the chocolate melts and the mixture is smooth. Stir in the Cabernet. Transfer mixture to a bowl and refrigerate until firm. Using a teaspoon or melon baller, form the mixture into balls about 1-inch in diameter. Roll in walnuts, cocoa powder or cappuccino powder.

About 30 truffles

WARM CHOCOLATE CAKE

Executive Chef, Jeffrey Reilly, The Duck Club Restaurant at Bodega Bay Lodge and Spa

15 ounces semi-sweet
   chocolate
15 ounces softened butter
10 ounces sugar

8 eggs
10 ounces cake flour
3 tablespoons cocoa
Vegetable spray

Melt the chocolate and let set until cool to about 90 degrees. Cream butter and sugar until light and fluffy. Add eggs one at a time, incorporating thoroughly after each addition. The butter will look "broken" after several eggs are added, this is normal. Add the melted chocolate and mix well. Combine the flour and cocoa. Add to the chocolate mixture, being careful not to over-mix. Spray 12 timbales with vegetable spray and fill with the chocolate mixture, knocking out air pockets and scraping top level. Freeze for at least 4 hours. Bake frozen at 375 degrees for 17 minutes, or until just set around the edges.

12 servings

PECAN PRALINES

Chef Tess Ostopowicz, GTO's Seafood House

1 cup white sugar
1 cup brown sugar (½ cup
   light and ½ cup dark)
1 pinch of salt
½ cup milk
2 tablespoons light corn syrup

2 tablespoons butter
1 teaspoon vanilla
1½ cups pecan halves, may
   substitute almonds or
   walnuts for a different twist

Mix sugars, salt, milk and syrup in heavy 3-quart pan and cook to a soft ball stage. Add butter and vanilla. Beat until cool. Add pecans and drop by tablespoon onto wax paper. When firm, store in closed container.

Approximately 2 dozen

CHOCOLATE-WALNUT PORT BALLS

Chef Robin Lehnhoff, Lake Sonoma Winery

1 cup walnuts, ground or finely chopped
1½ cups confectioners' sugar, sifted

2 cups grated bittersweet chocolate
4 tablespoons Lake Sonoma Zinfandel Port
Cocoa powder

Combine nuts, sugar and chocolate. Moisten with port to form a stiff dough. Form into small balls and roll in cocoa powder to coat. The warmth of your hands will help to melt the chocolate some to help bind the confection.

For best results with walnuts and chocolate, use a food processor to grind nuts and then use a cheese grater attachment (if you have one) for the chocolate. When mixing ingredients, use a paddle mixer.

Approximately 2 dozen

CHOCOLATE-CABERNET BROWNIES

Chef Robin Lehnhoff, Lake Sonoma Winery

1 pound semi-sweet chocolate, pieces or chunks
½ pound unsalted butter
1 cup cabernet sauvignon, reduced to 2 tablespoons

1 tablespoon vanilla extract
4 eggs slightly beaten
1½ cups granulated sugar
1 cup all purpose flour

Melt chocolate and butter in double boiler. Let cool slightly. In mixer, combine eggs and sugar and beat until fluffy. Add cabernet and vanilla. Add melted chocolate to sugar-egg mixture and blend well. Add flour and just fold in. Pour brownie mixture into sheet pan (9 x 12-inches) lined with parchment. Bake at 350 degrees for 25 minutes. Brownie is done when the sides look slightly dry and pull from edge. Do not overcook!! Cool completely before cutting. Best results happen when brownies are refrigerated and then cut.

2 dozen

MEYER LEMON OLIVE OIL CAKE

Chef Colleen McGlynn, Toscana Sonoma

5 eggs plus 2 egg whites
¾ cup sugar
2 lemons, zest only, finely chopped
1 cup flour
½ teaspoon salt

½ cup plus 1 tablespoon Gewürztraminer
½ cup plus 1 tablespoon DaVero Meyer Lemon Olive Oil

Separate the 5 eggs. Beat the egg yolks with sugar until light-colored and ribbony, about 4 minutes. Add the zest. Sift together the flour and salt and add to egg yolks. Mix well. Add the Gewürztraminer and olive oil, mixing thoroughly. In a clean bowl, beat the 7 egg whites until stiff peaks form. Fold into egg yolk mixture. Oil a 10-inch springform pan and line the bottom with parchment paper. Add the batter and bake in a preheated 325 degree oven for 55 to 60 minutes or until done. The cake will spring back to the touch and a toothpick comes out clean. Let cool before removing sides of pan.

Serve with fresh berries and berry purée.

1 10-inch cake

RUM KUGEL

Rum Balls

Chef Robert Buchshachermaier, Café Europe

7 ounces chocolate, grated
7 ounces hazelnuts or filberts, grated
3½ ounces powdered sugar

Dash of sugar
2 egg whites
3 tablespoons rum
3 tablespoons water

Place all ingredients in a bowl. Using your hands, mix into a solid dough. Form small balls. Roll in sugar and let dry for several hours. Store in a dry place.

Approximately 30 balls

WATERMELON GRANITÉ

Chef Jessica Gorin, **J** Wine Company

Suggested wine: **J** Sparkling Vintage Brut

3 cups watermelon purée   1½ cups simple syrup
2 cups **J** Sparkling vintage brut   (or mint simple syrup)
1 cup water

To make simple syrup, put equal parts sugar and water in a small pot. Bring mixture to a boil and then remove from heat. For mint simple syrup, add ½ cup mint leaves, roughly chopped, as soon as mixture is removed from heat. When syrup cools, strain out leaves.

For granité, combine all ingredients in a shallow pan and freeze. Scrape to serve.

The granité can be served before a main course as a refresher, or with fresh sliced fruits and berries for a summertime dessert.

SADDENED CHOCOLATE CAKE

Chef Matthew Bousquet, Mirepoix Restaurant

4 eggs   ½ pound melted butter
4 egg yolks   1¼ tablespoons plus
½ cup sugar   ¼ teaspoon flour
½ pound melted chocolate

Whip eggs, egg yolks and sugar until quintupled in volume. Whisk butter into chocolate. Then whisk in whipped eggs and sugar. Fold in flour, then cool. Yields 1 quart. Portion into 8 greased coffee cups (about 4 ounces each). Bake at 425 degrees in a convection oven for 8 to 10 minutes or until they no longer jiggle. Chill completely. Remove from cups and serve at room temperature.

8 servings

CHOCOLATE ORANGE ZUCCHINI CAKE

Andy's Produce Market, Kathrin Skikos

2 cups flour
1 teaspoon baking soda
1 teaspoon baking powder
1 teaspoon cinnamon
½ teaspoon nutmeg
½ cup unsweetened cocoa
¼ teaspoon salt
3 large eggs

2 cups sugar
¾ cup oil
2 cups shredded zucchini
¾ cup buttermilk
1 teaspoon vanilla
1 teaspoon grated orange peel
1 cup chopped nuts

Sift flour, soda, baking powder, spices, cocoa and salt. Beat eggs in large bowl. Gradually beat in sugar until mixture is fluffy and pale ivory in color. Slowly beat in oil. Combine zucchini with buttermilk. Stir flour mixture into eggs, alternating with buttermilk mixture. Beat on slow speed of mixer until combined. Stir in vanilla, orange peel and nuts. Pour into 2 greased loaf pans. Bake at 350 degrees for 30-45 minutes. Cool 10 minutes and remove from pans.

ORANGE GLAZE

2 cups sifted powdered sugar
3 tablespoons orange juice

2 teaspoons grated orange peel
2 tablespoons melted butter

Blend all ingredients until smooth. Pour on semi-cooled cakes.

2 loaf pans

PEANUT BUTTER CHOCOLATE CHUNK COOKIES WITH A GLASS OF CLOVER MILK

Chef John Stewart, Zazu

1 cup soft unsalted butter
¾ cup sugar
¾ cup packed brown sugar
1 teaspoon kosher salt
2 eggs
1 teaspoon vanilla extract

2 tablespoons water
1 cup creamy peanut butter
2 cups all purpose flour
1 teaspoon baking soda
1 cup semi-sweet chocolate,
    hand chopped into chunks

Preheat oven to 350 degrees. In an electric mixer, cream the butter, sugars and salt. Add the eggs and vanilla. Add the water and peanut butter. Add the flour and baking soda and stir until just combined. Stir in the chocolate chunks. Place scoops of dough on a baking sheet lined with parchment. Bake about 8 minutes, until edges are golden. We like to serve this warm out of the oven and under-baked alongside a big glass of Clover milk.

MEYER LEMON SORBET WITH GOAT "MASCARPONE"

Bodega Goat Cheese Requeson

Patty Karlin, Bodega Goat Cheese

1½ cups sugar
1½ cups water
1 cup Meyer lemon juice
4 ounces goat milk

1 4-ounce tub requeson
    (or crema)
1 tablespoon Meyer lemon zest
1 tablespoon gelatin
2 tablespoons water

Heat sugar and water in saucepan to dissolve sugar. Pour in bowl with lemon juice. Add milk, requeson and zest. Meanwhile combine gelatin and cold water, let rest for 5 minutes. Heat gently to dissolve completely. Add to above mixture. Freeze ice cream maker base, then add combined mixture and mix according to instructions.

1 quart

BREAD PUDDING

Chef Matt Schacher, Kenwood Restaurant and Bar

1 loaf cinnamon raisin bread cut in 1-inch pieces	1 cup sugar 10 egg yolks
2 cups cream	Zest of ½ lemon

Mix all ingredients together and pour into a baking dish or individual soufflé cups prepared with butter and sugar coating. Top with brown sugar. Bake at 350 degrees for ½ hour. Serve with butterscotch sauce.

BUTTERSCOTCH SAUCE

1 cup brown sugar	1 tablespoon lemon juice
¾ cup butter	1 cup heavy cream
¼ cup dark rum	

Melt sugar and butter together until well incorporated. Bring to a boil and add rum and lemon juice while whisking vigorously. Add cream all at once and bring to a boil. Take off stove and cool.

10 servings

WINDSOR'S CHERRIES CABERNET

Windsor Vineyards

2 pounds cherries, halved and pitted	3 tablespoons honey 2 teaspoons lemon juice
1 cup fresh orange juice	1 tablespoon fresh mint, minced
½ teaspoon cinnamon	
½ teaspoon orange peel, slivered	1 cup Windsor Cabernet
½ teaspoon fresh ginger, minced	Sauvignon

Mix all ingredients together. Cover and chill. Serve cold, garnished with whole cherries or a mint sprig.

4 to 6 servings

ORANGE AND ROSEMARY CRÈME CARAMEL

Chef Patrick Martin, Charcuterie

CARAMEL

2 cups sugar   Cold water to cover

CUSTARD

3 cups milk   6 whole eggs
5 sprigs of fresh rosemary   6 egg yolks
1 orange, zested and juiced   1¼ cups sugar
   (½ cup)

Cook sugar and water until caramelized. Boil milk, rosemary and orange zest. Let infuse covered for 15 minutes, then strain. Mix eggs, yolks, sugar, orange juice. Add strained milk and mix well. Coat 9 ramekins with the caramel, fill with custard and bake in bain-marie for 45 minutes in a 375 degree oven.

9 ramekins

PEAR FLAN WITH BRANDY

Chef Phil McGauley, Korbel Champagne Cellars

6 Anjou pears, peeled, cored   2 egg yolks
   and thinly sliced   1 whole egg
6 tablespoons brandy, divided   1 cup flour
⅓ cup plus 2 tablespoons   1 teaspoon lemon zest
   melted butter, divided   1 cup milk
½ cup sugar

Sauté pears in 3 tablespoons butter until soft. Add 2 tablespoons of brandy and sauté for 2 minutes. Butter 8 individual 8-ounce ramekins with 2 tablespoons of butter and divide the pears amongst them. Beat sugar, egg yolks and egg together until smooth. Beat in ⅓ cup butter, then the flour, the rest of the brandy, lemon zest and milk. Batter should be smooth. Pour the batter over the pears in the ramekins. Place the ramekins in a hot water bath and bake for 25 minutes or until gold brown in a preheated 350 degree oven. Serve with warm caramel sauce.

THE WEDDING LAVENDER
CRÈME BRÛLÉE

Chef John Stewart, Zazu

For our wedding, we had people throw lavender on us instead of the traditional bird seed, so we named this brûlée after the big day.

6 egg yolks
2 eggs
¾ cup sugar, plus more to
    brûlée

A pinch of kosher salt
1½ cups milk
2¾ cups cream
1 tablespoon lavender

Set up an ice bath for later. In a medium bowl whisk the yolks, eggs, sugar and salt together. In a medium saucepan on medium high heat, scald the milk, cream and lavender. Slowly whisk the hot cream into the egg mixture. Cool in a bowl set in the ice bath. Preheat the oven to 300 degrees. Strain the custard into ramekins and place the ramekins in a baking dish and surround with water half way up the sides of the ramekins. Bake the brûlées until set, about 50 minutes. Remove from the oven and refrigerate. To serve, sprinkle the top of each brûlée with sugar and use a torch to caramelize the top, spinning the brûlée and being very careful to caramelize the top evenly and not burn yourself.

12 brûlées

Sebastopol

Vella Cheese Building – Sonoma

Parham '88

Vella Cheese Company

The town of Sonoma's Vella Cheese Company may once have been a little known culinary secret, but not any more. Food critics nationwide have praised the broad range of cheeses made at the local creamery, and the business has been earning an amazing amount of awards for its products.

At the 2002 California State Fair, Vella cheeses won the following awards: Rosemary Jack, gold; Pesto Jack, gold; Habanero Jack, silver; Mezzo Secco, gold; California Daisy, bronze. At the 2002 Los Angeles County Fair, Vella won these awards: Toma, gold; Asiago Medium, gold; Mezzo Secco, gold; Monterey Jack, Rosemary, gold; Monterey Jack, Habanero, gold.

Vella Cheese also won a first place at the American Cheese Society's annual conference in Washington, D.C. for an original grating cheese called Romanello, available only at the store. Vella is also a former U.S. Cheese Champion for its Monterey Dry Jack-Special Select.

Open Monday through Saturday, 9 to 6
315 Second Street East
Sonoma, California, 95476
(800) 846-0505

J Wine Company

Balancing tradition with youthful exuberance, owner Judy Jordan explores the spirit of Russian River Valley winemaking with **J**.

One of the few vintage sparkling producers in California, **J** set the standard for méthode champenoise since its initial release. **J** has now expanded into still wine production with fine Pinot Noir, Chardonnay and Pinot Gris from seven estate Russian River Valley vineyards.

At the contemporary Visitor's Center, **J** has introduced a new form of culinary awareness, with its food and wine pairing program. The abundance of local, seasonal and organic foods is finessed into custom recipes created by **J**'s chef and kitchen staff.

11447 Old Redwood Highway
Healdsburg CA 95448
(707) 431-3646

Petaluma Coffee and Tea Company

This noted Petaluma coffee roasting company is conveniently located near downtown in Petaluma's historic warehouse district.

Fondly known as "the Coffee Company" among locals since 1989, the on-site retail store carries an extensive selection of full-leaf teas and tisanes, brewing accessories, and gifts. This warm, friendly store serves as a coffee roasting, wholesale, and shipping center as well as a sought-out retail source.

You are invited to stop in to watch the staff roast premium, organic and Fair Trade coffees. Open Monday through Saturday.

212 2nd Street
Petaluma, CA 94952
(800) 929-5282
www.petalumacoffee.com

Andy's Produce

Andy's Produce, an established Sebastopol institution, is truly a family affair. Three generations of Andy and Katy Skikos' family work hard to bring the absolute finest produce available to their Sonoma County customers.

Located on the outskirts north of Sebastopol, Andy's open-air market also features an extensive bulk grocery section, all natural health and beauty products, and a wide variety of gourmet wines and cheeses.

Besides Andy and Katy, three daughters, two daughters-in-law, and 12 granddaughters are involved in the business, and now a great granddaughter is at the market on a regular basis.

Andy's is not just about the women in the business. Two sons, a son-in-law, and seven grandsons are also involved in the company, which includes trucking. . And, to make the family connection complete, Andy's brother is also a member of the family produce team.

The produce stand was started 36 years ago and evolved with Sebastopol over the years. Considered to be one of the County's oldest and most successful family businesses, Andy's expanded into the wholesale business in 1993 to serve the fresh produce needs of a range of emerging quality restaurants in the area. For more than 36 years the family has insisted on operating a quality produce market that visitors and residents alike have come to expect. You are invited to enjoy the family's friendly and remarkable service while browsing through their remarkable selection of top-quality products.

1892 Gravenstein Highway North
Sebastopol, 823-8661

PEACH SMOOTHIE

Chef Clo

2 cups Clover buttermilk
3 cups peaches, peeled and
frozen (or sliced frozen
peaches or nectarines)

½ teaspoon vanilla
3 tablespoons brown sugar

Put all ingredients in blender. Cover and blend for 10 to 15 seconds.
Top with peach slice and a mint leaf.

2 servings

APRICOT SMOOTHIE

Chef Clo

1 cup apricot nectar
½ cup Clover buttermilk
¼ box silken organic tofu

1 medium banana
6 ice cubes

Mix in blender until creamy smooth. Top with a scoop of
Clover Vanilla Ice Cream.

ORANGE-BANANA SMOOTHIE

Chef Clo

½ cup Clover buttermilk
1 scoop Clover orange Sherbet

6 ice cubes
½ large banana

Mix in blender until creamy and smooth. Garnish with a dollop
of orange sherbet and mint leaves.

2 servings

PINEAPPLE-COCONUT FRAPPE

Chef Clo

1 cup pineapple-coconut juice (Knudsen)
½ cup Clover buttermilk

¼ box silken organic tofu
1 medium banana
6 ice cubes

Mix in blender. Top with 3 melon-ball scoops of Clover Vanilla Ice Cream or Clover lemon sherbet.

2 servings

MOCHA CREAM SHAKE

Chef Clo

4 teaspoons sugar
2 tablespoons instant coffee powder
½ cup chocolate syrup

2 scoops Clover chocolate ice cream
3 cups cold Clover milk

Combine sugar, coffee, syrup and ice cream in blender. Cover and mix at high speed. Remove cover and with motor running, gradually add milk.

4 servings

STRAWBERRY FROSTED

Chef Clo

1 pint fresh strawberries
⅓-½ cup sugar, as desired
2 cups Clover milk

1 cup Clover vanilla or strawberry ice cream
Whipped cream

Clean berries, reserving 4 for decoration. Force remaining berries through a sieve. Add sugar and chill. Add milk and ice cream and stir until ice cream is partially melted. Pour into glasses and top each serving with whipped cream and a whole berry.

4 servings

Kozlowski Farms - Forestville

Parkerson '96

Splendor
in the glass

OUR CO-SPONSORS

A heartfelt "thank you" is expressed to the following co-sponsors of Sonoma County - Its Bounty II.

RECIPE CONTRIBUTORS

*Recipes for this book were received
from the following Sonoma County Chefs:*

Brian Gerritsen, Applewood Inn & Restaurant, Guerneville

Liz Ozanich, Brasserie De La Mer, Vineyard Creek Hotel, Spa &
  Conference Center, Santa Rosa

Luca Citti, Café Citti, Kenwood

Robert Buchschachermaier, Café Europe, Santa Rosa

Michael Quigley, Café Lolo, Santa Rosa

Maria Belmonte, Caffé Portofino, Santa Rosas

Randy Hoppe, Catelli's The Rex, Healdsburg

Patrick Martin, Charcuterie, Healdsburg

Martin Courtman, Chateau Souverain, Healdsburg

Emile Waldteufel, Creekside Bistro, Santa Rosa

Bernadette Burrell, Dempsey's, Petaluma

Michael Ghilarducci, Cucina Rustica, The Depot Hotel,
  Sonoma

Vicky M. Walker, DoubleTree Hotel, Rohnert Park

Mark Purdy, Dry Creek Kitchen, Healdsburg

Jeffrey Reilly, The Duck Club Restaurant, Bodega Bay

Doug V. Lane, Equus, Fountaingrove Inn, Santa Rosa

Dan Dabbas, Essa's, Petaluma

Eve Litke, Farmhouse Inn, Forestville

Jesse McQuarrie, Feast, An American Bistro, Santa Rosa

Tess F. Ostopowicz, GTO's Seafood House, Sebastopol

Gary Chu, Gary Chu's, Santa Rosa

Christian Bertrand, Glen Ellen Inn, Glen Ellen

Graziano Perozzi, Graziano's Ristorante, Petaluma

Tai Olesky, Harvest Grill, Hilton Sonoma County, Santa Rosa

Jessica Gorin, J Wine Co., Healdsburg

Jan Rosen, J. M. Rosen's Waterfront Grill, Petaluma

Barbara Hom, Jellyfish, Sheraton Petaluma Hotel, Petaluma

Jeffrey Madura, John Ash & Co., Santa Rosa

Josef, Josef's Restaurant & Bar, Santa Rosa

Randy Lewis, Kendall-Jackson, Santa Rosa

Max Schacher, Kenwood Restaurant, Kenwood

Phil McGauley and Laurie Souza, Korbel Champagne Cellars,
and Robin Lehnhoff, Lake Sonoma Winery, Korbel

Roger Martial Praplin, La Gare, Santa Rosa

Manuel Azevedo, La Salette, Sonoma

Corey Basso, Le Bistro, Petaluma

Lisa Hemenway, Lisa Hemenway's Bistro, Santa Rosa

Jesse Mallgren, Madrona Manor, Healdsburg

Manuel Arjona, Maya Restaurant, Sonoma

Carlo Cavallo, Meritage Restaurant & Oyster Bar, Sonoma

Matthew Bousquet, Restaurant Mirepoix, Windsor

Dan and Kathleen Berman, Mixx Restaurant & Bar, Santa Rosa

Thanit, Pad Thai Restaurant, Santa Rosa

Randy Summerville, Rosen's Eastside Grill, Petaluma

Todd Muir, St. Francis Winery, Santa Rosa

Thomas Oden and Franco Dunn, Santi, Geyserville

Scott Snyder, Sassafras, Santa Rosa

Josh Silvers, Syrah, Santa Rosa

Derek McCarthy, Tastings Restaurant & Bar, Santa Rosa

Jiraporn Sujiva, Thai Cuisine, Petaluma

Dusky Estes, Zazu, Santa Rosa

Jeff Mall, Zin Restaurant & Wine Bar, Healdsburg

Recipes were also submitted from the following individuals and businesses:

Jeff Young, Alexander Valley Vineyards, Healdsburg

Katie Heing and Kathrin Skikos, Andy's Produce Market, Sebastopol

Angelo Ibleto, Angelo's Wine Country Deli, Sonoma

Patty Baker (Individual)

Patty Karlin, Bodega Goat Cheese, Bodega

Norma Poole and Joe Gentry, Cline Cellars, Sonoma

Dennis Hipolito, Cucina Paradiso, Petaluma

Gary Arthur, Flamingo Resort Hotel & Conference Center, Santa Rosa

Gina Gallo, Gallo of Sonoma, Healdsburg

Sondra Bernstein, The Girl and the Fig, Sonoma and Petaluma

Bob Engel, Gourmet Mushrooms, Sebastopol

Ken Tominaga, Hana, Santa Rosa

Jean-Claude Balek, Bayview Restaurant, and Carlo Galazzo, The Tides Wharf Restaurant, The Inn at the Tides, Bodega Bay

Carol Kozlowski-Every and Kimberly Every-Knechtle, Kozlowski Farms, Forestville

Kathy Young, Lombardi's Deli & Gourmet BBQ, Petaluma

Michele Anna Jordan

Heidi Kirkland, Oh! Tommy Boy's Organic Farm, Petaluma

Rodney Strong Vineyards, Healdsburg

Joe Peirano and Jose Perez, Semolina, Petaluma

Junny Gonzales, Sonoma Foie Gras, Sonoma

Laurent Manrique, Sonoma Saveurs, Sonoma

Larry Peter, Spring Hill Jersey Cheese Co., Spring Hill Farm, Petaluma

Timber Crest Farms, Healdsburg

Christine Topolos, Topolos Russian River Vineyards Restaurant

Toscana Sonoma, Da Vero, Healdsburg

Miranda Luddy, Vella Cheese Co., Sonoma

Lee and Shirley Walker, Walker Apples, Graton

Windsor Vineyards, Healdsburg

Sonoma County... Its Bounty II

64 Jessie Lane, Petaluma, CA 94952

Please send _____ copies of **Sonoma County – Its Bounty II** $27.50 each _____
      California residents add sales tax $ 2.06 each _____
      Postage and handling $ 4.00 each _____
      Total Enclosed _____

Name _____

Address _____

City _____ State _____ Zip _____

_____ Check or money order enclosed

Make checks payable to *Clover Stornetta Farms*. Mail to Ellen D. Moorehead, 64 Jessie Lane, Petaluma, CA 94952. Profits will directly benefit social, environmental and agricultural endeavors through Community Foundation Sonoma County.

Sonoma County... Its Bounty II

64 Jessie Lane, Petaluma, CA 94952

Please send _____ copies of **Sonoma County – Its Bounty II** $27.50 each _____
      California residents add sales tax $ 2.06 each _____
      Postage and handling $ 4.00 each _____
      Total Enclosed _____

Name _____

Address _____

City _____ State _____ Zip _____

_____ Check or money order enclosed

Make checks payable to *Clover Stornetta Farms*. Mail to Ellen D. Moorehead, 64 Jessie Lane, Petaluma, CA 94952. Profits will directly benefit social, environmental and agricultural endeavors through Community Foundation Sonoma County.

Sonoma County... Its Bounty II

64 Jessie Lane, Petaluma, CA 94952

Please send _____ copies of **Sonoma County – Its Bounty II** $27.50 each _____
      California residents add sales tax $ 2.06 each _____
      Postage and handling $ 4.00 each _____
      Total Enclosed _____

Name _____

Address _____

City _____ State _____ Zip _____

_____ Check or money order enclosed

Make checks payable to *Clover Stornetta Farms*. Mail to Ellen D. Moorehead, 64 Jessie Lane, Petaluma, CA 94952. Profits will directly benefit social, environmental and agricultural endeavors through Community Foundation Sonoma County.